Praise for *Smarter, Faster, Cheaper*

"State-of-the-art nuts and bolts for the modern marketer."
—**Seth Godin, author,** *Linchpin*

"A great read for passionate entrepreneurs looking to market their businesses by inspiring, educating, and entertaining."
—**Tony Hsieh, #1** *New York Times* **best-selling author of** *Delivering Happiness* **and CEO of Zappos.com, Inc.**

"In his smart and practical book, David Siteman Garland shows how to deploy your personality, passion, and knowledge to turbocharge your marketing. This no-nonsense guide will help entrepreneurs large and small spread their message and build their business."
—**Daniel H. Pink, author of** *Drive* **and** *A Whole New Mind*

"David is energy, passion, and execution rolled into one package. Bet against him at your peril. David Siteman Garland is a *trust agent* and future king."
—**Chris Brogan,** *New York Times* **best-selling author of** *Social Media 101* **and** *Trust Agents*

"David brings to business marketing some things essential to your success: motivation and passion. The stories and lessons shared here are rich with real advice wrapped in vitality and proven through experience. Take this book and go earn your success!"
—**Brian Solis, author of** *Engage! The Complete Guide for Businesses to Build, Cultivate, and Measure Success in the New Web*

"If you love to spend buckets of money on traditional ads and you can't wait to cold call sales prospects, then you don't need this book. But if you're looking for no-nonsense ideas on reaching buyers, then read this book right now. It's a fast read because Garland is non-boring."
—**David Meerman Scott, best-selling author of** *The New Rules of Marketing and PR*

"If you're into boring marketing books, take a pass—this book reads like an enthusiastic success coach urging you to greatness."
—**John Jantsch, author of** *Duct Tape Marketing* **and** *The Referral Engine*

SMARTER,
FASTER,
CHEAPER

SMARTER, FASTER, CHEAPER

NON-BORING, FLUFF-FREE STRATEGIES FOR MARKETING AND PROMOTING YOUR BUSINESS

DAVID SITEMAN GARLAND

WILEY

John Wiley & Sons, Inc.

Published by John Wiley & Sons, Inc., Hoboken, New Jersey.
Published simultaneously in Canada.

For general information on our other products and services or for technical support, please contact our Customer Care Department within the United States at (800) 762-2974, outside the United States at (317) 572-3993 or fax (317) 572-4002.

Wiley also publishes its books in a variety of electronic formats. Some content that appears in print may not be available in electronic books. For more information about Wiley products, visit our web site at www.wiley.com.

Library of Congress Cataloging-in-Publication Data:

Garland, David Siteman.
 Smarter, faster, cheaper : non-boring, fluff-free strategies for marketing and promoting your business / David Siteman Garland.
   p. cm.
  ISBN 978-0-470-64792-9 (hardback); ISBN 978-0-470-93379-4 (ebk);
  ISBN 978-0-470-93380-0 (ebk); ISBN 978-0-470-93381-7 (ebk)
 1. Marketing.   2. Industrial promotion.   I. Title.
  HF5415.G35 2010
  658.8'02–dc22

                                                                2010028570

Printed in the United States of America.

10 9 8 7 6 5 4 3 2 1

To the love of my life and my perfect puzzle piece, Marcie, for being the reason I'm excited to wake up every day.

To my mom, Nancy, for always encouraging me to pursue my dreams, love, and for being my personal editor/best Mom ever.

To my dad, Randy (aka "Tron"), for his cheerleading, inspiring support, and being the world's best Dad.

Contents

Acknowledgments

This is definitely the most awkward portion of the book because I know I might miss someone, so I'll keep it brief. This is really a big thank-you to everyone who made this book possible. My mom for being "my personal editor"—even though sometimes she edits and then accidentally deletes those changes and suggestions. Lauren Lynch, Linda Indig, and everyone at John Wiley & Sons for taking a chance on a young author. Marcie for not complaining when I spent many a Saturday in a coffee shop to work on the book (and for her loving support). Inspiration from some of my favorite authors, entrepreneurs, and big thinkers including Seth Godin, David Meerman Scott, Chris Brogan, Daniel Pink, John Jantsch, Brian Solis, Tony Hsieh, and many others. Encouragement always from my friend (and attorney) Jeff Michelman who has helped me immeasurably since I first got into business. The hundreds of guests on *RISE*, friends online and off (a shoutout to everyone on Facebook and Twitter), the *RISE* community of entrepreneurs that keep me going, all of my family, and you.

About This Book

When you break down all the fluff, there are two ways to promote and market your business: **dumber, slower, and expensive—or smarter, faster, and cheaper.**

Today's approach to marketing creates a substantial advantage for entrepreneurs. For the first time since the oldest business transaction in history—when early man traded fashionable animal skins for dinosaur—**the barriers to successful marketing have crumbled.**

Now the Davids of the world actually have an advantage over the Goliaths.

Not only has the Internet become the great equalizer by giving scrappy entrepreneurs the same tools that are available to big brands and major companies, but it has shifted what is important when it comes to marketing and promoting, creating an incredible opportunity for entrepreneurs. **Now, it takes far less money, but more passion, more personality, more creativity,** and the opportunity to *become a trusted resource* and the go-to person, as opposed to a *sketchy product pusher.*

Smarter, Faster, Cheaper is a living breathing buffet of **non-boring, fluff-free ideas**, and strategies, as well as stories and takeaways from successful entrepreneurs (including author and entrepreneur David Siteman Garland) so you can take advantage of this unbelievable opportunity, whether you are an entrepreneur, solopreneur, freelancer, or forward thinker ready to innovate.

It is time to stop trying to out-spend and instead time to out-educate, out-hustle, out-give, out-connect, out-care, out-inspire, out-create, and out-help the competition.

Introduction

When you break down all the fluff, there are two ways to promote and market your business: dumber, slower, and expensive—or smarter, faster, and cheaper.

Dumber, slower, expensive is essentially the way it has always been taught: You market the *product*. Your job as an entrepreneur, business owner, or marketer is to get as many people as possible to buy by shoving whatever you've got down their throats.

Perhaps your product is the fastest, the coolest, the cheapest, the most expensive—or the most mediocre (which I'm sure yours isn't). Or maybe your services are the best in the world. You realize, of course, that a product isn't just limited to a physical entity—like a plastic moose head or something of the sort. It is whatever someone else is buying. It can be services, software, virtual material, yourself (as in the service/expertise you might provide in a given field), donations . . . whatever.

The thing is—product pushing is freakin' expensive. It can be pretty pricey to buy traditional ads, hire spokespeople, work with PR and marketing firms still stuck in 1982, and so forth; so this expense meant mass appeal was the way to go. Cast a wide net and see who fell into it. Potential customers were everywhere. And if they did not need the product, the strategy was to create a need and sell, sell, sell. Those who had the means with a mega marketing budget were assumed to be the most impressive.

Or you could hire a spokesperson or PR rep and hope your product was interesting enough for some delicious media attention that would encourage people to buy. Or hey—how about a website? You design a website for which the goal is to convince browsers to buy, buy, buy. Or you position yourself within social media and broadcast your message (as opposed to being helpful) with the same end in mind: Sell, sell, sell.

This didn't provide much opportunity for hustling entrepreneurs and forward thinkers like us. Goliaths had the advantage, not the Davids (awkward David pun not really intended, actually).

But here's the thing—and chances are, you already know this: We have all gotten wise to the product pushing. Unless you have a marketing budget with a TON of zeros, it can get frustrating.

There *has* to be a better way, right?

The answer is the smarter, faster, cheaper approach (who saw that coming?). As opposed to product pushing, this method is based around becoming a trusted resource, an authority figure, someone who others like and trust. *Not* someone who talks down to potential customers but someone who brings people together by being helpful.

The smarter, faster, cheaper approach includes creating (or getting involved with in other ways) valuable content (text, video, audio, and/or speeches/workshops)—both online and off—that is focused on educating, inspiring, and/or entertaining. It also means that you have to consciously focus on one-on-one relationship building (online and off) with a mentality of giving, and in many cases you can use your content as a handshake. It is a change in focus from leading with your product to leading with *you*. This new-school approach isn't about becoming a better marketer but instead redefining how we look at marketing and promoting. Because this type of marketing and promoting doesn't taste or look like marketing and promoting (you know, that "ewwwwww" feeling) but instead builds trust, relationships, and you guessed it: sales. Becoming smarter, faster, cheaper goes way beyond just creating content. It extends to everything you do and how you approach business and marketing—especially in this increasingly transparent business world where people can reach hundreds or thousands or millions of people with a click of the button (thank you, social Web!).

Because if you think about it, everything is marketing in some shape or form (explicitly or implicitly). Forming relationships with others is essentially marketing yourself. Customer service is marketing because in the social Web age, good AND bad experiences are shared instantaneously. Allowing people to get to know you is marketing. Helping people is marketing. Your online reputation is marketing. What are people saying about you? Who you associate with and who knows you is marketing. This new era of business creates all kinds of unique opportunities when it comes to marketing, PR, and even rethinking advertising (the big "A" word and, yes, there ARE smarter, faster, cheaper ways to advertise).

What You'll Get Out of *Smarter, Faster, Cheaper*

The idea here is to spark your imagination. It's to help you tap into your creativity by learning from successful, unique people who share their secrets, struggles, and tips. Of course, the end goal is to take action. Without this, we just have a bunch of ideas in our head or on paper.

Do you have to do *everything* in this book to be successful? C'mon now, you know the answer to that. My aim is merely to share with you ideas, real-world examples, and personal experiences from which to draw. I'm not saying you shouldn't spend a million dollars on banner ads for your business if that is what you want to do; by all means, go for it! I *am* saying there is a new way to market and promote businesses (and yourself) that is just coming of age—and now is an amazing time to join this movement.

The bottom line is that our consumers, clients, customers, and friends are all smart, and the changes in marketing happening now are going to position us and our businesses for success now and way into the future. Meaning you are forming long-term relationships as opposed to a one-night stand.

Why am I telling you this? Honestly, because with enough passion, determination, and willingness to be yourself AND build a business—pretty much anyone can do what I've done and many of the folks throughout this book have done—and you can do it in your own way. It doesn't take a superhuman. It doesn't take some kind of rocket scientist tech genius. It doesn't take someone of a certain age or personality type. Sure, some will fail, but not us. Not the hustling innovators and forward thinkers who genuinely care.

Sure, this is a book about business. However, it's not an old-school business book, or one whose goal is to convince you how amazing the Internet is, or a personal brag fest of I-did-this-and-you-should-do-exactly-what-I've-done-or-you-are-a-dumb-dumb. There are no charts or graphs, no stuffy case studies, and no complicated "higher math." This is a book filled with ideas, stories of successes and failures, advice from trusted resources, and a buffet of marketing options that come from the perspective and experience of hustling entrepreneurs (both myself and many others). Hopefully, it is as entertaining as it is informative, and hopefully, you'll find some interesting marketing strategies (as much as I hate that word) that will work well for you and your business. (Then again, you might read one chapter and regift the book or use it as a coaster.) Either way—I hope it proves useful in some manner.

Who This Book Is For

Supershort answer: You.

Short answer: Forward-thinking entrepreneurs, free-lancers, solopreneurs, savvy marketers, and business owners looking to innovate. Not just stay afloat, but thrive. Be the *best*.

Long(er) answer: Anyone who has something to promote and market, and is willing to think differently. And it can be ANYTHING—really. It can either be an existing or future product. It might even be that you are interested in marketing yourself. Perhaps you already know what passion you want to turn into a business and you aren't sure how you will make money from it yet. Or maybe you're promoting services, doing advertising and sponsorships, or attracting investors. Whatever it is—this is for you.

Let's begin by assuming that your products and/or services are amazing (after all, I don't think anyone starts a company or creates a product with the goal of making something mediocre). Because even the most stellar and creative marketing in the world doesn't make up for crappy stuff. If, at the end of the day, your product or service doesn't work or deliver—then smarter, faster, cheaper marketing will sink it just as fast as it could make it rise.

It doesn't matter if you are a pro at marketing and promoting or just getting going. Nor does it matter if marketing and promoting keeps you up at night with excitement because you love it or you cry yourself to sleep because you hate it. There is value at every level. *Smarter, Faster, Cheaper* is designed for forward thinkers—both young and young-at-heart. And it doesn't matter if you are a tech expert or tech confused.

Maybe you've started your tenth company or are thinking about starting your first. Or maybe you're thinking about innovating within your business and rolling out a new product, idea, or service. Perhaps you are a freelancer who stuck it to the man and is now out hustling and building your own business. You might simply be trying to grow your business or look for an edge.

Perhaps you're currently working for a company and are thinking about taking a plunge into the entrepreneurial pool. Maybe you're looking to build a brand that lasts; are a personal brand or "solopreneur" looking to generate more business; or (yikes!) a big brand looking to think smarter, faster, cheaper. Or you are a marketer who has noticed that your target market seems to have disappeared. Where the heck did they go and how do you reach them?

Now—who is this book NOT for (an equally important distinction)?

Anyone looking for a get rich quick scheme. This book isn't for you, so please hand it to someone else. Established business and marketing principles have been around for decades and building businesses and brands today still takes hard work, risk, patience, dedication, resilience, and a bit of luck (okay—sometimes a lot of luck). While "faster" in the title is key, it is based upon the idea of nimbleness and creative hard work—as opposed to an easy way out. No way around it: It takes time to be successful.

This book is not for those looking for an exact road map or a how-to book. Why? Because there *isn't* a road map. In fact, this is *why* we are all entrepreneurs—because we want to make our own maps, right? If there's one thing I've learned from personal experience, hundreds of interviews, and thousands of conversations, it's that entrepreneurs learn and do things differently. If you tell us what to do, we won't do it. We do it our own way. HOWEVER, if you share experiences, stories, and lessons with us, we can pick out the juicy nuggets to use for our business. This book is meant to be a source of ideas and inspiration based on real life as opposed to fluffy bunny theories taught by someone who hasn't experienced it. Some things will work for you, and others may not—but I can promise that everything here is based on experience, success and failures, both my own and others'.

This book is not for Negabots. You know the type. They are the ones who, when it is 85 degrees and sunny, complain that it isn't 86 degrees. Negabots find the worst in everything. The glass isn't even half empty—it's not worth drinking out of at all. They're often characterized by a lack of wanting to try new things, and a fixation on the way things were. They have excuses aplenty.

What You Can Expect

The big ideas and principles in this book aren't arrived at by simply throwing Mama's spaghetti at the wall and hoping a few pieces stick. I've brought in the big guns through a series of over 150 interviews conducted over the past three years. I've spoken to big-time entrepreneurs, creative thinkers, unique business people, crazy marketers—in short, people who are living their passion every day, are massively successful, walk the walk and talk the talk. These are people we can learn from because they really have tasted it by being smarter, faster, cheaper. Because learning from the best is always a great way to be inspired (and then you can always do it your own way if you prefer). These people include:

- Founder of Wine Library and author of *Crush It,* Gary Vaynerchuk.
- *Trust Agents* author and blogging thought leader Chris Brogan.
- Bravo TV's Millionaire Matchmaker, Patti Stanger.
- Social media all-star Sarah Evans from Sevans Strategy.
- Shama Kabani, president of Marketing Zen Group.
- Ali Brown, founder of Ali International.
- Tech thought leader and one-man media empire Robert Scoble.
- Brian Scudamore, founder of 1-800-GOT-JUNK.
- Scott Ginsberg, "The Nametag Guy."
- Best-selling author and founder of Squidoo, Seth Godin.
- Founder of Smart Bear Software, Jason Cohen.
- Steve Garfield, author of *Get Seen* and one of the original video bloggers.
- CEO of Zappos, Tony Hsieh.
- Author of *Never Eat Alone*, Keith Ferrazzi.
- Founder of Help A Reporter, Peter Shankman.
- Former creative head of Anheuser-Busch, Bob Lachky.
- Jason Fried and David Heinemeier Hansson from 37 signals.

- Jessica Kim from Babbaco.
- Sports networking czar Lewis Howes.
- Jason Sadler from IWearYourShirt.com.
- Timothy Sykes from TimothySykes.com.
- Dan Schawbel, founder of Personal Branding Blog.
- Brian Halligan, Dharmesh Shah, and Mike Volpe of Hubspot.

And many others are sprinkled throughout the book. Some you might have heard of (but not in this way, as I've personally interviewed them all as opposed to rehashing their theories), and others you might not have. What I found through speaking with these people and so many others were stories filled with inspiration, ideas, and lessons from which we can all benefit.

In addition to the stories and lessons learned from these individuals and companies, I've gathered valuable material from speaking and helping forward thinkers face their challenges and adapt to this (insanely) quickly changing world. I've been very lucky to have thousands of conversations in person, online, and at speaking events with marketers, big brands, niche brands, entrepreneurs, and business owners who have offered their perspective. These conversations are important because they represent an extremely wide range of opinions and experiences—from start-ups that are just getting cranking to seasoned entrepreneurs. Even those outside the entrepreneurial spectrum have had wonderful ideas to offer. After all, sometimes inspiration and ideas come from odd sources. When was the last time you had a great idea in the shower?

Plus, there are some personal examples from being in the trenches and building my brand, The Rise To The Top, to the number-one non-boring resource for making your business smarter, faster, cheaper (www.therisetothetop.com). This includes a web show for entrepreneurs and forward thinkers, articles, resources, tips, tricks, interviews, and much more. I firmly believe that you have to practice what you preach—and so, I've tried everything in this book. Plus, as an entrepreneur who has started three companies and tried everything under the sun to promote and market them, I've gotten to taste remarkable successes, crushing failures, indispensable learning experiences, and tons of takeaways. However, this book isn't about me. It is about you. So, what this has all led to is a book filled with stories, principles, and strategies to help you market, promote, and grow your business by being smarter, faster, cheaper.

Without further ado, let's get it rolling (or reading). You know what I mean.

1

The Shift

Finding Those Eyeballs and Big Mouths

Imagine that you have the greatest product ever. (And maybe you do!) Perhaps it's some kind of software. Or a product line. Or maybe it's simply your own expertise. You have developed it whatever it is—and now you need to *sell it,* one way or another.

To be successful, you need eyeballs—which are attached to people, who buy things (simple, right?). People have the tools to make their big mouths heard. The more passionate of these will not only know, like, trust, and purchase from you— but will also tell everyone *they* know about you. As one of these people myself, I can attest to the effectiveness of this method. If I get excited about something, I try to spread it like wildfire.

But not all eyeballs are created equal as far as your business is concerned. You want to reach folks who are genuinely interested in what you are marketing—right? You are probably aware of the more traditional ways of capturing eyeballs:

TV, radio, print (newspapers and magazines), billboards (seriously?), and setting up booths at trade shows. But are these the most effective?

The location of your customers' eyeballs is changing. Whether your customer is an 8-year-old schoolgirl or a 77-year-old retiree, eyeballs are increasingly moving online. It is no secret that consumers of all ages are shifting their attention from mainstream, traditional media to the far more active and evolving world full of blogs, social media (what I like to call the social Web), search engines, online video, and other appealing places.

Even more importantly—people are becoming more social and interactive. Social media usage is up and the social Web—offering the ability to connect one-to-one with friends, businesses, and so on—is here to stay. Sure, not everyone is taking part quite yet—but I would bet that a growing percentage of your target market is (especially if your marketing is skewing toward Generations Y and X). The point here is that the social subset of your market—the people who spread interesting stuff and open their big mouths—are a key component to smarter, faster, cheaper marketing.

Furthermore, there is no online marketing versus offline marketing today; it is both. The Internet has become a platform that amplifies what any one person could do in real life and these efforts build on one another. And it isn't just folks with zillions of friends, followers, and authority who are influencing opinions. These social tools allow nearly everyone—including me and you—to have *some* form of influence over our friends and connections and also become a trusted resource: the go-to person. The friendly and approachable expert. When you reach the passionate few, they spread the word for you.

Take, for example, mediapreneur Peter Shankman's HARO (Help A Reporter Out), a free service that sends multiple e-mails a day to anyone who subscribes with a list of reporters/journalists looking for experts and trusted resources. If you feel you are the right fit, you can respond and pitch the reporter. HARO has over 100,000 subscribers and has turned over a million dollars in profit ... in less than a year (and recently sold). It is an incredible free resource whose popularity caught on because of people being social and interactive. What happened was pretty simple—when you break it down.

1. Peter started HARO as a Facebook group. He had connections with reporters and simply shared stories they were looking for with others. In essence, he created high-value content for people and gave it away.
2. The group grew organically as people told their friends about it. For example, if you saw that a reporter was looking for a "cat expert" for a story, you might forward that query on to your friend who knows everything in the world about cats.
3. The group eventually got too big for Facebook and is now an e-mail service. Revenue comes from sponsorships, and Peter has been propelled to stardom—all for being nice and helping people by doing something he liked to do and turning it into a business model.
4. Peter has become a sought-after speaker, expert, and consultant based around his experiences. When he talks, people listen. This has opened up all kinds of incredible opportunities for him.
5. Possibly the most important thing here is Peter isn't a jerk face. He is approachable, and, while he is an expert, he doesn't pretend to be better than anyone else or act

like some kind of closed-off person that you can never get a hold of. He is a smarter, faster, cheaper trusted resource who connects with people one-on-one online and in real life.

A key part of the story takes place in the early days with that first group of people who helped spread the word. The social Web made it easy for them to do it, and by getting the word out about HARO, these people become even more well liked and trusted by THEIR friends. Why? Because they used their big mouths to help other people. It created a perfect triangular marketing and promotion situation. HARO was beneficial to people who were quoted in the media because of it. They told their friends who appreciated the tip as it could help them. And each time it got passed on, it grew. People were being helped, a profitable business was created, and Peter became an influential, trusted resource. I bet that you can create your own group—big or small—of similarly super-passionate people who spread things YOU create that help both them and others. The Internet has evolved to allow this to happen.

Of course, the Internet is not just confined to computers anymore. As we all know, mobile phones have become a significant hub for many people. Just how many is "many"? According to a report by Futuresource Consulting Senior Market Analyst David Luu called *Handheld Device Convergence,* within the next three years more than 1 billion people will have Internet access on their phones—and that number is expected to continue to rise. Tablet computing—using tools like the newly introduced iPad from Apple, which reportedly sold two million of the devices in just the first two months—is another option for the other-than-computer Internet user. Even our old forgotten friend the television is streaming shows from online via set-top boxes and through the TVs themselves. In essence, the Internet has become a syndicated platform that's spreading widely and deeply to nearly every demographic.

And with this shift and the evolution of the Internet, the one-way conversation has developed into a two-way conversation. Consumers have become mini-media sources who interact online and spread both positive and negative impressions and observations to their network in a variety of ways. Marketing has become a dialogue—one filled with personality and fun. Yes, believe it or not—business can be (and should be) fun.

This is somewhat of a frightening idea for companies that are obsessed with control and maintaining the status quo—the Goliaths of the business world. But for scrappy entrepreneurs, business owners, and passionate folks like us, this shift is amazing. It's allowing marketing to grow as a collective, interactive, and experimental medium as opposed to a tightly controlled message or "campaign." Now you can create your own media (video, audio, text, photos) and focus on one-on-one relationships with customers, your community, and new media sources.

The playing field has finally been leveled. Entrepreneurs, small businesses, and freelancers have the same tools available to them as multimillion-dollar corporations. Lean companies are at a distinct advantage in the new world of business building, marketing, and promoting, because they aren't required to ask a board of 739 people before posting something online (or going to the bathroom). Finally, David has been given a slingshot and can outmaneuver Goliath.

You don't have to be an *über*nerd-techie to maximize your position in this new era of business and marketing. It really doesn't matter if you don't know the difference between a megabyte and a spider bite—because the tools are there to help you grab those eyeballs, make connections, and market your business successfully.

Which begs the question: How has this new Internet-crazed era shifted entrepreneurship, marketing, and promotion? What has really changed?

Old School versus New School

These are the principles and practices that used to matter or were universally perceived to be true:

Mass appeal. Everyone was a potential customer or client.

Experience and credentials (master's degree, PhD, anyone?) mattered more than **passion and creativity**.

Big start-up bucks were a requirement—groveling before banks and investors mandatory.

Ginormous marketing budget and team were key. The more people hustling and dollars spent, the more dollars earned, right?

You were **only a trusted expert or resource if you had 50 years of experience**, wrote 30 books on the subject, and lived on a secluded mountain. And **these experts were not approachable or social** (they had no interest in interacting with plebeians like you and me). In fact, they were often downright mean and pretentious.

Only a **polished individual** with the look of a runway model should be the company's spokesperson. Or professional actors. (Personally, I would rather watch a sock puppet promote a product.)

Jerks and bullies dominated the business game. Throw enough people under the bus for your personal gain and you win.

High-budget productions created by a crew of 17 union workers was the only way to tell your story through video. Television commercials and (just kill me now) infomercials also got the job done.

The **entrepreneur's personality** was never the center of the approach. Why did it matter? Face of the entrepreneur? Who cared?

Geeks with their shiny gadgets and new toys were considered to be **a waste of time**, a flash in the pan, and people to avoid.

Websites that were either one-way, boring tech or corporate speak—or offered lots of flash but no content—were the accepted norm.

Experimenting and failing was a bad idea. Really, really bad and expensive. And if you did try something new, you never, *ever* talked about failures.

The world was considered a sinister place, with **competitors lurking everywhere**, plotting to steal or destroy your business. You had to be smart and suspect everyone. All competitors must be destroyed (insert evil laughter).

Social media was for kids with a minimum of three piercings. Or for huge, international brands that had the major bucks to maximize it.

Advertising was confined to 30-second radio and TV spots and static ads—print, online banner ads, billboards, the occasional bus stop. The company controlled the message—whether the customer was listening, watching, or even interested.

The ability to **suck up to traditional media for coverage** would make or break a business (yikes—where's the dignity in that?).

Blogs were for bragging about a company, sending out press releases, or for existential 20-somethings to tell the world about their relationship breakups and favorite music.

Businesses were conducted either online OR offline. Mixing the two? Insane! More important, offline businesses were for old-school corporate folks; online businesses were for the tech kids.

Big brands were the best teachers. We were to study how they were marketed and learn from them. Copy them. *Worship* them. Long live Goliath!

And a final old-school philosophy:

Never give away ANYTHING for free. Ideas, advice, products, and so forth. After all—we make these things so that people will *buy them*. How dumb can you be?

The Game Changer

The Internet. It has changed how and where people spend their time and money. It's shifted eyeballs from traditional media like print and television to the wondrous, wacky world of online content, full of niche (not mass) blogs, video, and new media with an emphasis on passion first. And with this change come new business models, new ways to market and promote—and a new way of thinking about entrepreneurship and business as a whole.

There has NEVER been a better opportunity to build, market, and promote a successful business. The tools are available to just about everyone. There's never been a better time to market like an entrepreneur and be the David and outhustle Goliath—no matter what your business is.

However—this doesn't mean that it takes any less work, passion, drive, and chutzpah. It doesn't mean suddenly you will be an overnight success just because you have an amazing idea and a website; and it also doesn't mean that face-to-face relationships are a thing of the past. A virtual handshake still can't replace a real-life one, and human connections are just as important as they ever were.

It *does* mean that opportunities—to create, to market, to reach and attract the right customers and clients, to build a like-minded community and audience—has been democratized. It means that increasingly more people have the chance to be interactive, social, and experimental, and to be successful on new terms—*our* terms.

The good news is that it takes far less money to reach infinitely more people than it did in the days of Henry Ford. But it takes MORE creativity, MORE passion, and much MORE speed and nimbleness. It takes an entrepreneurial approach to communicating in a focused, productive way.

Now, here are the NEW ways to market and promote your business:

Niche matters. The goal is to appeal to a specific, passionate, subset of people. We don't need to sell to everyone. In fact, if we do—we might want to rethink our game plan. We don't need millions of customers and clients to have a successful business. Instead, we can focus on the RIGHT customers and clients.

Money follows passion—not the other way around. Think about that for a second. Opportunity matters, but if we don't love what we're doing to earn a buck, the chance of financial failure is much greater.

We are **media sources**, not product pushers. You have the right to spread your message through whatever means you'd like—and unlike with traditional media, you can do so in a social and interactive manner. We can write like a magazine, create audio like a radio show, and even have our own TV channel if we want to—all for a fraction of the cost of traditional media. It's even better if we manage to gain full control of the creation of our content.

Expertise is relative and you don't have to be discovered or be a jackass to become a trusted resource. There is a new realm of trusted resources who are friendly, knowledgeable, and create their own media. They are approachable and not afraid to show their flaws. Perfection is overrated.

Genuine relationships matter—both online and offline. Who we know and who knows us (and how) is a giant piece of the entrepreneurial puzzle.

New media sources (bloggers, video bloggers, online content providers) in your niche can have a more substantial effect than the traditional kinds. Not only do they have passionate audiences, but they're able to reach people all over the planet . . . and can attract traditional media coverage.

In the increasing transparent business world, **nice, helpful people win**. Uncaring jerks are exposed either by Google or other people.

Passion trumps age. Whether they're 14 or 94, entrepreneurs who *care* all have an equal shot at marketing their businesses smarter, faster, and cheaper.

We are savvy, **and we listen to those geeks** when we want to know about the newest techie stuff. We know when to consult someone who knows more about a subject than we do.

Content is king. Marketing is the queen. Our website is our throne.

Experimenting with marketing ideas is now far less expensive. While trying and failing used to mean losing major dollars—or even your reputation—a bad blog post or idea are now just cheap learning tools. Get over it and move on!

Creativity wins. As Daniel Pink says in his book, *A Whole New Mind: Why Right-Brainers Will Rule the Future,* and as *Linchpin* author Seth Godin claims: Those who can think like artists are becoming the best entrepreneurs.

Your **unique personality** and presence matters. Forget the expensive spokesperson with the $200 hairstyle. We want to hear from *you*. The entrepreneur. The creator. It doesn't matter what you look like as long as you're genuine and passionate—and know what you're talking about.

Video is a great way to tell your story—no Hollywood budget or professional actors required. All you need nowadays is an idea, a platform, and a pocket camera costing a hundredth of the price of traditional fancy cameras to get you started. You might even want to start your own online show.

Understanding and participating in the social Web is vital. The tools are going to change; that is a fact.

But online, two-way communication between you and your customers, your clients, your partners, media sources, bloggers, and each other (entrepreneurs have to stick together, after all) are only going to keep growing.

Don't get me wrong; there are many fundamental business principles that have been around for decades that still hold true. For example, word of mouth has been around since early caveman recommended his club over his friend's hunting stick. **The Internet didn't invent word of mouth.** But it sure has amplified it!

There are **innovative solutions to advertising**— approaches that live, breathe, and spread like a 30-second or static ad never could. The rise of sponsored content is continuing to impact the advertising world—for a fraction of the cost of traditional campaigns.

We no longer solely control the message. Our consumers, clients, new media sources, and bloggers do, too. We become as much participants as we are creators.

The two-way website is replacing the one-way snoozefest. It's social, interactive, and filled with useful content (perhaps a mix of text, audio, and video). It's focused on educating, entertaining, and inspiring— not just selling, bragging, and showcasing.

Web design matters. A good design sets you apart from the pack.

Overnight success? When does that happen, really? But by marketing your business smarter, faster, cheaper, you're going to get there quicker. But, it takes time, effort, and patience.

Big brands might actually be the WORST companies to learn from. In fact, they have a thing or two to learn from us, the hustling entrepreneur!

The more we give away—whether it's content, education, or inspiration—**the more we get back over time.** But you have to know when to give and when to charge for your product or service. After all, you *do* want to make a profit, right?

2 | Create Your Foundation

Be a Human, Not a Company

Before jumping into strategies and ideas, let's chat a bit about foundation, because while tactics are fantastic, without a foundation, strategies and ideas will do nothing for you.

If there is one thing I've learned through hundreds of interviews and personal experiences, it is that both online AND offline marketing—and promoting the smarter, faster, cheaper way—is always the most successful when the focus is on a combination of being helpful and one-on-one human interaction. It's not an interaction between a company and a person, or a brand and a person. The Internet allows you to *scale*—or talk to many people at once—and still have it feel intimate. Social media and online video (or audio and text) facilitate this one-on-one conversation. It is the difference between showing up at a cocktail party and working the room (and not JUST talking business) versus sending a cardboard cutout of your nifty print ad to market and promote your business. One is human; the other is impersonal.

And while a virtual handshake doesn't equal a real-life one, it is an amazing way to reach out and make an impression. And who knows? We might run into each other at an event. We might talk for five minutes about sports, business, media—whatever. And while we go our separate ways at the end of the conversation, we can continue our interaction online.

The online world really isn't that different from the offline world—and you have to actively participate in both. You can't have your intern monitor your social media accounts—any more than you can have him or her show up for a meeting or lunch on your behalf—if you want to reach out and form relationships with new people.

Online exchanges are not about shoving your message down peoples' throats—and you wouldn't do that offline, either. Both rely on making connections, creating content (more on that later), and of course, selling a killer product/service (we all have to make money, right?).

Here is the funny thing: The Internet really isn't all that complicated. If you weed through all the clutter and confusion, the Internet is made up of just three things:

1. **Content**: Text, video, photos, audio, and so forth.
2. **People**: Visiting websites, social networks, forums, e-mailing, searching, and tweeting. At their computers. On their mobile phones.
3. **Products.** Virtual products and actual products. Things—*anything*—for sale.

If you combine all three, you have a winning formula in this new era of smarter, faster, cheaper brand-building and marketing.

Entrepreneurs versus Big Brands

Entrepreneurs and forward-looking thinkers have an advantage over big brands—both online and off.

Scrappy entrepreneurs and big brands are two different animals. While everyone can learn from each other, we are talking about some substantial variations here—some that can create problems when entrepreneurs try to act like big brands and vice versa.

For example, you might take a look at the websites and social media accounts from big brands like Starbucks or Southwest Airlines. Why? Because they are visible brands. And logically, some of us might try to follow in their footsteps and try to copy them.

In my opinion, however, these are the WRONG folks to emulate—because big brands are *very different* from scrappy entrepreneurs like us. Not better or worse, just different. Big brands have their own ways of doing things. They use expensive tactics, report to big boards, and keep huge advertising and marketing firms on retainer. They have lots of checks and balances. We don't. And the funny (and sort of ironic) thing is—that creates a BIG advantage for us.

Although some of these are generalizations, they are based on real conversations and experiences. Of COURSE some big brands act smaller and more nimble online (Zappos rocks). And clearly, some entrepreneurs try to act like big brands (which usually doesn't work).

What do you think is the number one advantage that big brands (and in many cases pre-Internet celebrities) have over small online organizations? There's really only one: built-in recognition and reach. And this recognition usually comes from offline activities—maybe stores or a boatload of traditional advertising. There are exceptions, of course, such as the big online brands like Google and Amazon, for instance. Recognition also comes over time; these companies weren't built overnight.

Perhaps you guessed "money" or "budget" as the advantage. However, I would argue the contrary. The problem with using a big marketing budget online is that it's a waste. You can buy traffic, but you can't buy *relationships*. Without a big budget, you have to be creative and focus on making one-on-one connections, networking, helping people, and, of course, ultimately running a successful business through the sale of something.

Online advantages for entrepreneurs are so abundant that an entire book could be written on that subject alone. It is easy to be human when you are an entrepreneur—and even easier to show your passion and personality. It's much less complicated to make decisions and take action. Without a board of directors to whom you're forced to report, you don't need a group of advisors to sign an agreement about posting something on your blog. You can out-create as opposed to out-spend, out-hustle, out-care, out-teach, out-connect, and out-help the competition. When you are smaller, it's fairly straightforward for people to know you, like you, and then, ultimately, buy from you. Goliath-like brands do not care what you had for dinner last night, what your kids' names are, or how much you love your favorite sports team. Goliath just wants your money (insert evil laughter here). Later on, we will definitely be diving into the forgotten art of small talk.

You can work smarter, faster, and cheaper when *you're* your own business. Plus, of course, you can experiment without the risk of losing tons of money. Try something and it doesn't work? Oh well. You can learn from it and move on. In short: The best companies have a face and personality online *and* off. And the social Web has created a huge advantage to being David as opposed to Goliath, allowing the little guy to outmaneuver as opposed to outspend the competition.

Passion, Personality, and Knowledge

It all starts with passion, personality, and knowledge. Gary Vaynerchuk is just one of those guys who exudes passion, personality, and knowledge, which has led to him being the go-to person in his niche. I mean, he OOZES it. For those of you who've never heard Gary's story—here is the CliffsNotes version:

Gary's father came to the United States from Belarus and began working at a little liquor store. It is one of those classic stories where, over time, his dad went from stock boy to manager to part owner to owner of Shoppers Discount Liquors in beautiful, exotic New Jersey, which eventually evolved to Wine Library. Along came Gary, who took the company to the next level via online marketing—which translated to over $50 million in sales.

But then something funny happened. Gary turned 30, woke up, and freaked out. He realized that he wasn't 100 percent happy with what he was doing with the company, and he wanted to share his knowledge of wine, which he had built up from experience and reading. So he had his assistant buy a $500 video camera and started taping a 20- to 30-minute daily wine show. It was just as quirky as Gary himself, and it showcased his knowledge of wine and his personality.

What exactly do I mean by quirky? Well, for starters this isn't your grandfather's formal wine show. Gary has a chalkboard behind him that he uses to write random slogans on. He spits his wine into a New York Jets spit bucket, and often has an unusual cohost. A smattering of old-school Worldwide Wrestling Federation figures have been known to join him at his table. Gary didn't wait for someone to come and crown him a "Wine Expert"; instead, he created his own platform to demonstrate his knowledge. And his personality, passion, and knowledge led to recognition of his expertise and Gary becoming THE go-to person in the wine world.

Fast-forward to over 900 shows later—and Gary has become a phenomenon. More than 100,000 people tune into *Wine Library TV* daily, which led to an appearance on Conan O'Brien's late night talk show where Gary convinced Conan to eat dirt. His story landed him a book deal, and his first book, *Crush It!,* became a best seller. Gary also does short videos on his website, GaryVaynerchuk.com, that are related to business and the Internet. He also launched a massive consulting firm called Vaynermedia. That's quite a few accomplishments for a guy under 40.

Despite the many platforms through which Gary makes himself known, I didn't know what to expect when I made the trek—and trust me, it was a trek—to Wine Library in New Jersey to interview Gary. Would I get the same personable guy that I saw on his shows? Or would he be very different off camera than he was on? One can never be too sure about these famous personalities, after all. But I hoped for the first option—to encounter the genuine, friendly, energetic guy I saw in the media.

And lo and behold . . . I absolutely did. Gary's energy was the same. His charisma was the same. *Gary* was the same. The brand and personality that he conveyed wasn't an illusion. I didn't feel like I was meeting an actor or a character; Gary is a person. And more than anything, he genuinely cares—about his business, his family, and other people. In fact, Gary—a consummate salesman and hustler—somehow managed to sell me six books when I was there interviewing him.

But what separates Gary from many other business owners isn't a huge brain—although he is both intelligent and street-smart. It isn't some business school formula that he learned to run businesses. Rather, it is a perfect storm of personality, passion, and knowledge.

The Whuffie Factor author Tara Hunt told me once during an interview that Gary essentially gets away with more promoting than most people *because* he is so passionate and excited—like a little kid. And because he cares so much, everyone around him begins to care more.

So what does this mean for all of us entrepreneurs?

It used to be that passion, personality, and knowledge didn't matter unless you were some kind of celebrity-in-training trying to get "discovered." Instead, most companies focused just on money, as opposed to expertise and trust, and had a faceless brand pushing products. Let me ask you: Who is the founder of Pepsi or GM? They don't seem to be very visible anywhere. But today's smarter, faster, cheaper brands *do* have visible AND approachable founders who aren't just leaders; they are trusted resources.

The perfect storm for marketing smarter, faster, cheaper includes three qualities:
1. Passion
2. Personality
3. Knowledge

And these qualities go together like a full outfit; if you are missing a piece, it just won't work. They go hand-in-hand-in-hand and are the basis for everything in smarter, faster, cheaper. You hold the power to create expertise. You hold your own destiny to become the go-to person in your niche. You don't need permission.

Passion Is Contagious

Let's start with passion. Every person has a passion—and so do the best businesses. What are *you* passionate about? Baseball? Fashion? Cooking? Old cars? Contemporary art? I'll bet you can talk enthusiastically and engagingly—for a pretty long time—about whatever it is that excites you most. It's REALLY obvious in some cases when you're talking to someone about his passion, whereas some are far less obvious. And it doesn't matter if you are an extrovert or an introvert; in fact, even if you *are* a more naturally withdrawn person, I'll bet your passion gets you going. You may not start doing cartwheels, but your excitement barometer does go up—noticeably. If you think about it, we talk about things we are passionate about *naturally*. We are *happy* when talking about, partaking in, or are somehow connected to our passion. We get other people excited; though it is cliché, it's true: Excitement is contagious.

Passion somehow creates focus. Even if we are ridiculously attention-deficient and jumping from shiny red ball to shiny red ball, passion is our entrepreneurial Ritalin. Boring chores like doing the laundry, carpooling the kids, and fixing stuff around the house somehow doesn't seem so bad when you are pumped up on passion about other parts of your life. Think about those dreary, mundane business tasks that we have to do. Filing. Collecting payments. No fun, right? But being driven by passion truly makes them a whole heck of a lot easier to do.

When you combine your passion and business, you create the perfect storm that suddenly makes everything seem a lot better. You are excited to go to work and to finish that project you're working on—even if it's late. It makes you go above and beyond.

And passion goes way beyond products. It has a higher purpose. Let's say you sell toasters (I know, random). You might be superpassionate about the toaster itself. We all know that somewhere, someone is the toaster king and thinks about toasters morning, noon, and night. But, perhaps you are passionate about something bigger than toasters. You are passionate perhaps about healthy eating. Or eating hot foods. Or you are passionate about making people laugh, so inside each toaster you sell is a small, funny booklet of 100 things NEVER to toast.

Another real-life example comes from Tony Hsieh, founder of Zappos and author of *Delivering Happiness*. The Zappos story is everywhere, so I will spare you the long version. The short version is that Tony has built a brand and company to more than one billion dollars in sales with a passion focused on caring, customer service, and a fun company culture. His passion isn't focused on the product (which is shoes and expanding into other areas as we speak). When I asked Tony what he is passionate about, the product didn't come up. Instead, he talked about how he likes to be excited to go to work everyday—hence, the fun culture at Zappos—and how he enjoys starting things and entrepreneurship, as well as his zest for customer service. Here is some food for thought: When you see Zappos EVERYWHERE (on TV, in magazines, online, offline, whatever), folks aren't talking about the shoes. They aren't talking about the cool, new, red Reebok sneakers. Instead, the buzz is about the company: How incredible their customer service is. How unique and interesting Tony is. How fun the tours are when you visit Zappos headquarters. How they give $2,000 to people after training to NOT take the job. Do you think it is a coincidence that the stories and buzz that spread are directly related to Tony's passion? I don't think so either.

Money follows passion—not the other way around. Just think about it: Passion sells. It creates caring. It promotes and markets. It keeps you going when things get tough. Passion builds business and creates community—because people want to spend their time with passionate people. You don't try to spend time with dreary, apathetic people—do you?

Passion can transform the ordinary into the very interesting and buzzworthy. For example, I once hosted a party at my house because I won a prize at an event: an evening with a chocolate expert. Now, upon first glance that may not seem very interesting. You eat some chocolate, and that's about it—right? But, the chocolate master (which I call him), was *insanely* passionate about chocolate. He didn't have what I would call a HUGE personality (like Gary Vaynerchuk), but he was incredibly enthusiastic and gave a fantastically detailed and interesting presentation. And guess what? We told our friends about how great he was. Oh—and by the way—he owns a chocolate store where we now regularly buy chocolate.

If we, as entrepreneurs or marketers, can't be excited about our product, service, or company, how can we expect anyone else to be?

Personality: Yes, You Have One

Have you ever seen a mismatched couple walking down the street holding hands? Maybe she's a knockout, gorgeous model type, and he's a cross between Mini-Me and Uncle Fester. Of course you have. Now—despite the fact that this is a little shallow—let's be honest here. In all likelihood, your friend leans over to you, and—in reference to the less-aesthetically pleasing person—says, "He must have a great personality."

Why? Because personality matters. Online and offline. In life *and* in business.

And personality is in the eye of the beholder. Some people might think you are really funny. Or very blunt. Or a straight shooter. Cocky. Loud. Introspective. Quirky. Bossy. Serious. Wacko.

You might be any of these or a variety of other personality types or others. There is no denying, however, that your personality is one thing that defines you and sets you apart from others. It would be safe to conclude that absence of personality does not attract others. Who wants to listen to or watch someone with no personality? I, myself, would rather watch my socks dry.

So, what does this have to do with marketing and promoting by being smarter, faster, cheaper?

Simple. The foundation of your business—your products, expertise, and services—is *YOU*.

It used to be that you could—or had to—hire someone to speak for you and your business. You hired a PR company to craft a message or spin something when there was a fiasco. Or you signed a wind-blowing-through-the-hair actor. Or you commissioned a press release. These actors are hired for a reason; they represent everywoman/man. They are often chosen to be the most likable or represent a certain demographic. They're meant to blend in, so the company shines.

The problem with this, of course, is authenticity. It is really hard to be authentic when the person or piece of paper delivering your message isn't you. Consumers nowadays want the *real* you—quirks and all.

When you blend in—you don't stick out. You aren't memorable. You won't spark conversation online or offline—regardless of the kind of company you run.

Everything discussed in this book needs a face. And that face has to be you. People want to hear from YOU. The CEO. The founder. The creative genius. The leader. The trusted resource.

Of the hundreds of entrepreneurs I've interviewed, the very best people running the show are in the public eye. They are genuine. They are visible. And the coolest part about it? They all have REALLY different personalities. And they don't depend upon hard pitches or carefully crafted scripts.

If you let it, technology is bringing us together—on social networks, blogs, and with other tools like never before. But despite all of these advances, one age-old principle still holds true: People do business with people they know, like, and trust. Your customers want to see your face and share their interests with you.

Now, this doesn't mean that as the owner, founder, CEO, president, emperor, czar, or whatever important title you have that you must handle every minute detail. Being visible doesn't mean that people expect your voice on the other end of the phone 24-hours-a-day, 7-days-a-week. It doesn't mean that you can't hire help or outsource certain things (although outsourcing relationships probably isn't recommended). It doesn't mean you can't ask for help. It doesn't mean that once you are gone, your hard work is gone. Legacy and personality are allowed to mix. You can scale yourself. Some of the top personality-driven brands and businesses have found ways to scale to build more of a legacy (the brand lives on beyond you). For example, author of *Never Eat Alone* and *Who's Got Your Back* Keith Ferrazzi preaches the power of building business relationships. The brand is very much him. He speaks, consults, writes, and so on. He scaled his personality-driven brand by creating Ferrazzi Greenlight, which is a unique company that takes his philosophies and trains others to teach them. They now have other people besides Keith who speak and consult. That is just one example of many when it comes to scaling personality.

Now, there are a few misconceptions when it comes to showing our personalities. There might be that little part of your brain—the negative part—that perks up with a stern shaking finger and rears its head every so often with a bunch of "Yeah, buts . . ." or "That will never work, because. . . ." For this reason, I polled business owners and entrepreneurs with simple questions and discovered their biggest misconceptions relate to making themselves accessible to their customers. The data I've gathered comes from social networks, events, real-life conversations, and my website. So, without further ado, here are some common misconceptions about adding personality to your business.

I Don't Have an Outgoing Personality

This is a big one. The truth of the matter is you don't need to have star power or resort to crazy antics to have the type of personality to which people are drawn. Think about it. I'm sure there are more than a few people you like who are really quiet. Or good listeners. Or eccentric. Tony Hsieh is the very visible and key driver of the Zappos brand and he is (somewhat) quiet, reserved—and represents his company like a rock star.

I'm Not Polished Enough

First of all, what the heck does that mean? To me, *polished* is synonymous with *rehearsed*—which flies in the face of the notion of authenticity. Polished also screams "perfection"—and you certainly don't have to be perfect. You can misspell something in a tweet, and the world won't end. You can stumble a bit in a video. And guess what? People will like you more because you are showing you are a human. Not a robot. Not an actor. A PERSON. Just like them.

I Don't Want My Name Everywhere or to Be that Accessible

Not to perpetuate any stereotypes here (especially since I'm respectful of all generations), but this is a big problem with some Gen Xers and baby boomers. Ask any 15-year-old who grew up with Facebook and you will get a blank stare in response to this concern—or Gen-Y entrepreneurs who, in the words of my good friend The Nametag Guy Scott Ginsberg, "stick themselves out there" without fear of being stalked. Accessibility doesn't mean you are giving someone the keys to your house or the right to call you at 2 A.M. It doesn't mean that every little detail about you is going to be made public. Google yourself. Do you like what you see? If not, becoming more visible is going to help. Plus, it will help you understand that your online reputation matters a lot. In the increasingly transparent world we are living in, it is almost like everything you do might be on video and available for the world to see. This isn't meant to scare you, but just to state the truth of the matter. The good thing, in my opinion, is that transparency creates more authenticity and makes the world a better place.

My first TV experience was in 2008 when my show, *The Rise To The Top*, hit the airwaves in St. Louis, Missouri, on ABC. Though I'd been on TV before, I had never written my own show or worked with a teleprompter or a crew. Looking back on the first season, I had one HUGE problem: I tried to be someone else. I'm not really sure who, but it definitely wasn't me. I tried to act like what I thought a "TV person" should be. I was forcing it, spray tanned (I know—stop laughing) and stiff as a board.

The lesson here is I didn't use my authentic voice and tap into my true personality. It took a couple of years before I started feeling *really* comfortable just being myself.

But the funny thing is that as soon as I started being myself—and took the risk of relying on my own personality everywhere (social media, videos, my website)—things took off. Web traffic soared. My connections and network expanded unbelievably. Our community of entrepreneurs and business owners grew by 2,000 percent. My content became more captivating and memorable—because it was quirky like me. And it has laid the foundation for the future.

If you have passion for your business, you *will* be able to get people excited about it—case closed. That's it. No need to read any further. Go grab a drink and watch some cable. (Just kidding.)

Expertise: It's All Relative

Close your eyes for a moment and picture an "expert." What did you see? A guru on a mountaintop who sits in silence for 23 hours a day? Or perhaps someone who is really, really, really old? Or a polished (oh, there goes that word again) pundit who contributes to countless television shows? Author Malcolm Gladwell claims in his great book *Outliers* that expertise and mastery is attained after 10,000 hours of practice, whereas other people claim you are an expert only when someone else deems you to be one.

Despite these differing notions of what an expert is, I bet you are an expert at *something*—or can be considered a trusted resource—or a thought leader—on a specific subject. I'm sure you know more than me—and a LOT of other people—about something. And you can begin doing this right now. You don't need permission (coming up are ways you can share and spread this expertise).

Realize that back in the day (pre-social Web days where it was difficult to create and promote your own content on-line) there was a fairly vast separation when it came to entrepreneurs and thought leaders. Experts and entrepreneurs were two separate categories. Entrepreneurs built companies and sold products. Experts offered commentary on TV and radio and maybe wrote a column. Each had his own business model. Entrepreneurs sold products, services—whatever. Experts sold themselves and maybe products associated with their expertise like DVDs or books. Now those categories have blended, and there is an incredible opportunity to be both the entrepreneur and the thought leader.

It used to be that in order to become an expert, you had to be *discovered*. You had to pitch traditional media and maybe if you were lucky or good looking enough you would land some kind of TV deal. Or if you were an amazing writer you could land a syndicated column. Plus, the term *expert* was synonymous with "all knowing." This meant flaws were hidden and perfection was held in higher esteem than authenticity. But, success stories are often needles in the haystack. The barrier to entry was high and things took forever. For example, you had to get past gatekeepers, a.k.a. decision makers, who decided if you were good enough or not. Good looking or not. Smart or not. The right fit or not. And the gatekeepers controlled you. They told you what to say and what your schedule was. They controlled the platform and how you reached your audience. You had to play by their rules. Plus, your expertise had to be broad enough to reach a mass audience. Too specific was a problem. Contrast that now with specific being an advantage, because there is unlimited opportunity to laser cut your niche online whether you are looking to rally together pony lovers, green entrepreneurs, or grandmas who bake cookies. Now, the gatekeeper is you. The tools are available for you to show your knowledge and build community.

The definition of expertise, and perhaps the word itself, has changed, since oftentimes the word "expert" makes people think of someone who calls themselves an expert and is a jerk. Let's go with a new phrase: trusted resource There are many ways to create it, show it, and monetize it all by being smarter, faster, and cheaper as well as social, interactive, and experimental. A trusted resource isn't all-knowing. It is okay to have flaws (we all have them, right?), and be real. Being a trusted resource might be showing your knowledge and helping others. It might be learning along with people and sharing those findings. It might be becoming a trusted resource by association by surrounding yourself with good company and helping others. It isn't just about being a pundit.

What is the definition of a smarter, faster, cheaper trusted resource?

First, you have to walk the walk or at the very least be walking while talking. What have you done that you can help others with? On what topics are you a walking encyclopedia? Having the personal experience gives you instant credibility. Timothy Sykes (more on him later) is one of today's most influential financial bloggers with a booming business. What qualified him to advise others? He did it himself first. He did—THEN he taught. He also does WHILE he teaches. These are two important qualities.

Second, you have to *know* the walk and talk. I love the example here of professional athletes. When tuning into a St. Louis Cardinals baseball game, I sometimes hear the announcers talk about certain players who are real "students of the game." They study baseball just like Gary Vaynerchuk studied wine. They watch film of themselves AND others. They love the game and keep up to date. Learning is a life-long process. Plus, sharing things you learn and picking the brains of others builds credibility and authority.

Third, you must know what you know and know what you don't. If you've never built a 100-million-dollar company, why pretend to be an expert at it? Stating what you know from your experience is critical; stating what you *don't* know is equally important. It doesn't mean you are a failure if you don't know something (heck—there are SO many things I don't know about). It just means that you can focus on the things you DO know—the things that you have a unique experience and take on. After all, trying to be a trusted resource on everything is really not being a trusted resource at all.

Fourth, you have to talk the talk and bring people together. This isn't done just by literally talking. This is done by writing, helping, facilitating, and educating others, and effectively communicating your ideas. You can create the content on your own and bring like-minded people together both on- and offline to form a community led by you. It isn't about having a brag fest or talking down to people; it is about you *helping* others, and, of course, understanding who you are talking to. For example, perhaps your expertise is in product design. You probably aren't targeting Steve Jobs at Apple to give him advice on how to design a product. But, perhaps you are reaching out to college kids looking to launch a product but having no idea about design. Or perhaps you bring together young designers looking to learn the business and all of you can learn from each other. It is all relative.

Fifth, you must leverage your talk (much more on this later). What can becoming a trusted resource do for your business? Short answer: everything. People buy from people they trust and like. People help people they trust and like. Media sources love trusted resources for guest articles, videos, and so on. Would you rather buy from a faceless company or a trusted resource who happens to have a product that fits your need? However, calling yourself an expert or trusted resource? Bad idea. *Other people* calling you an expert or a trusted resource? Fantastic idea! By showing your passion, personality, and knowledge, you can encourage others to promote and market you and your products and services.

Bottom line: Whatever knowledge and expertise you have can be used for something much more powerful than making yourself the center of attention. It can bring people together and propel your business forward.

3 | Become a Trusted Resource

Because Nobody Cares About Your Product

Now, despite what we've covered so far—just making yourself visible and acting as the face of your business—doesn't mean that everything—or really, anything—is about you. It's about your customers. Your clients. Your potential clients.

Here is a harsh reality (eloquently mentioned in David Meerman Scott's *The New Rules of Marketing and PR* . . . I guess Davids with three names think alike): Nobody cares about our products. People care about themselves, solving their own problems, being liked perhaps, and so on. But that is okay. This isn't a bad thing. It simply requires a shift in thinking from "product pusher" to "trusted resource"—and that creates a big opportunity. This doesn't mean your product is NEVER mentioned or plugged, it just means, in a manner of speaking, that when you shake someone's hand online or off, you aren't leading with the product. The product comes later.

By far, the number one repeated mistake that business-people make when marketing and promoting online (and offline) is to talk—excessively—about themselves . . . and how amazing their product is. The "brand-new features" that are the best in class, the really "cool" new desk chair their company purchased, or a press release about how the product or service is now available in Outer Mongolia. Really riveting stuff.

This is why many websites and most corporate blogs (and business-related blogs in general) fail; these companies don't create material that is focused on the consumer. Instead, they make it about themselves. If you want a bullhorn, you can buy a billboard, right?

Why do people consume, participate, and engage with online content (articles, videos, audio, photos) and offline content (seminars, speeches, workshops)?

Usually it is to:

- Solve a problem.
- Be entertained.
- Learn about something they are interested in.
- Get a little inspiration.
- Pass the time. (Hey, we all get bored. You know it's true.)

The path to success lies in your ability to become a *resource* for others on a particular subject about which you are passionate. It could be a functional, educational resource or an interview series with leaders. Or it could be your talent for sharing funny musings. But it's *not* being a product pusher. It's acting as a soft seller who creates valuable content and . . . "Oh, *by the way*—I have this amazing product/service/thingy you might be interested in learning more about."

Your role as a resource starts with your capacity to understand exactly what interests your customer or potential customer (insert whatever word you want in here: fan, community member, client) in relation to your product. It doesn't matter if you are selling to businesses, consumers, or Basset Hounds.

For example, let's say that your company manufactures hockey sticks. Your potential customers and niche clearly would be interested in hockey. The mistake here would be to create a blog or video series or podcast series focused on how awesome your sticks are. Who cares? A better move would be to center your website around hockey-related content: interviews with NHL players, top tips for shooting a puck harder, other hockey-related resources that your users might need, or short videos showing off trick shots. The list goes on . . . you get the point. And although you, of course, have your product information on your site and clearly mention the fact that you sell sticks, the site is created around something interesting and useful to your audience. It is a *soft sell*.

Now, replace hockey sticks with "*literally anything*"—and there you go. Realize this content positions you as a resource online and off. You become the go-to person. And go-to people can speak at conferences, conduct seminars, and accrue all the benefits accorded to someone looking to help people. It is marketing by educating, entertaining, and inspiring.

There is a tremendous opportunity for every entrepreneur, solopreneur, and company to create buzz around their expertise and become a trusted resource that is much bigger than just the individual and his business. If you are a fitness trainer, for example, you wouldn't write a blog about your buff body and how awesome your personal training sessions are; you wouldn't push people to buy, buy, buy. Instead, you'd be much better off providing fitness tips, demonstrating various routines on video, interviewing clients about their own experiences, and so forth.

The more personality-filled, specific, interesting, and useful your content is, the more people will be attracted to it. If someone likes your content, there is a good chance they will like the other products and services you have to offer. Why? Because great content will allow people to know, like, and trust you. You can check off all three by jumping on the content train. Toot. Toot.

There might not be a better example of marketing "around the product" than software company Hubspot. It is much more than a software company. I'd argue it is 50 percent a business that sells a product and 50 percent media source creating valuable content. Building a business and creating content is the new walking and talking. Started by Dharmesh Shah and Brian Halligan, Hubspot's main product is software, which it sells to people who are looking to attract visitors and users to their websites. As you can probably guess, the software industry is, as they say—and I'm putting this lightly—somewhat crowded. Lots of people sell all kinds of software you may or may not need. Brian and Dharmesh could have gone the traditional marketing route. Buy old-school ads. Pitch to software magazines. Yadda, yadda. . . .

However, the pair took control of their own marketing and instead became a *media maker, creator, and source.* They decided to be helpful educators—not aggressive salesmen—to their target market. They and their growing team do this by:

- Updating (usually several times a day) their Hubspot Internet Marketing Blog—a site that offers all kinds of tips, tricks, and studies.
- Producing *Hubspot TV*, a live, weekly, online TV show where the hosts tackle topics related to inbound marketing and tech.
- Hosting a whole series of webinars that people can attend to learn about hot topics in the field.
- Creating a plethora (yes, I just used the word plethora—be impressed) of free, incredibly helpful tools. For example, they offer a Website Grader that takes a comprehensive look at your website and gives you a grade based on tons of criteria, as well as a personal report if they so choose.
- Writing a book. Yup, a good old-fashioned book (just like this one). *Inbound Marketing* came out with a bang and offers tips on attracting customers using the Hubspot methods.
- Having folks from the company who are trusted resources and personalities in different areas speak at conferences. They don't pitch products but rather *educate* the crowd. (I know this from personal experience, since I attended one of these conferences and was definitely impressed.)
- Making their content available everywhere, shared by people all over the place. On social media sites. At real-life conferences and events. Picked up by search engines.

Oh, and here's a fun fact: All of this amazing content is **free** to consume (well . . . except the book, of course, but that won't break the bank). Free as in costing nada, nothing, zero. But note in the preceding examples that all this free content is

NOT focused on their product. It is focused on helping and educating others. And which of the following do you think sounds better to someone who is interested in generating more leads on their website?

1. "Buy our amazing Hubspot software, and it will help you generate leads!"
2. "Tune in this Friday to *Hubspot TV* where Mike and Karen will answer your questions about generating leads."

Hmmmm . . . Captain Obvious at play? It is SO much easier to promote and market helpful content to your online community as opposed to pitching products.

So, you might be wondering—how does giving stuff away for free generate business? Obviously, at the end of the day, you have to make money and sell *something*. You can't make a house payment, put gas in your car, or get your eyebrows waxed if you don't make some kind of money.

Hubspot tackles this by offering all kinds of gentle reminders about its product to lead you from becoming educated to becoming an actual customer. Brian and Dharmesh aren't afraid of mentioning their product, and they certainly don't pretend they have nothing to sell (that would be a bad idea). However, they do so honestly AFTER they have educated and inspired you. It isn't a hard sell like a late-night infomercial.

Examples of some of these gentle reminders are:
Displays: Both the Hubspot website and various blog posts provide links to find out more about what the company offers by redirecting users to its product pages. It isn't shoving product in people's faces; it feels

more like a trusted friend saying, "Oh, by the way, in case you are interested, we have something great that's available for you to buy."

Mentions: Brian and Dharmesh use opportunities like webinars, the occasional *Hubspot TV* piece, their book, and so forth to discuss their products. As Mike Volpe, VP of marketing at Hubspot, told me, they try to abide by at least a 90/10 rule (or maybe 85/15). The higher percentage of content is focused on education. The lower percentage is focused on the pitch. Your results will, of course, vary.

It's sort of like going into a wonderful, free art museum that markets to art enthusiasts and those who want to learn more about famous artists and their works. They stroll through the galleries and enjoy the art. They take a tour. They learn something during a free class. And oh, by the way—there is this nice gift shop (signs clearly marked) where they can purchase something to take home. Or a place to make a donation (a membership desk, perhaps). Marketing around the product clearly works—*artfully* so. (I couldn't help it. So sue me.)

As a result, we—and countless other users—genuinely like and trust Hubspot. It has become more than just a software company; it is a highly valued resource. The site influences users who view Brian and Dharmesh as trusted resources (which they are). They become buzzworthy and interesting to write and talk about. They have even expanded and hired journalists and a staff that just creates content all day. And their revenue is *way* up.

Talk about doing things cheaper! Nothing Hubstop does to market its products costs a fortune. Creativity. Commitment. Smarts. Don't those sound like talents you already possess?

4 | Selling Sucks

To Educate, Inspire, and Entertain Is Fun

Scott Ginsberg, "The Nametag Guy"—who has made a living from wearing a name tag and inspiring people (seriously) through books, seminars, products, and more—said it best: "If people like you, they will buy everything you have."

What gets people to purchase your product? The quick sell is going the way of the dinosaurs; it used to be the norm to try to force this on potential customers. Many salespeople genuinely believed that they only had 30 seconds or a one-quarter page of advertising to get their message across. They told people what would happen if they used your product: They would attract members of the opposite sex, keep up with their neighbors, and be invited to all the fun parties. All you had to do was buy what they were selling.

That approach doesn't work so well anymore.

I'm not suggesting that direct marketing is dead; it isn't. But I *am* suggesting that the smarter, faster, cheaper way is to view sales as a long-term goal—not a quick, manipulative, pushy attack.

Educate, Inspire, and Entertain

If you give educational, inspirational, and/or entertaining content away—with your number one goal being to help people—your business will flourish. If you give it away *just* for the sake of selling stuff—it will be obvious. And this isn't fluffy theory; we are all smart. We know when we are being hustled by people with manipulative intentions (shudder). It is the difference between watching a really bad movie and a good one. A good film entertains and captures your attention. A bad one leaves you cranky and feeling like you wasted your money.

The amazing thing about online and offline content and becoming part-business/part-media source is that there are all kinds of paths that can lead to an eventual purchase of your product but there are other HUGE long-lasting benefits as well.

I Don't Have a Product Yet!

You may not have anything to sell yet—so can you still benefit from creating your own media, publishing, and trusted resource model?

Absolutely!

In fact, sometimes this is an even greater opportunity— because the world of possibilities is essentially yours.

Here comes another hockey example (stop groaning! Hockey is a great metaphor for business ... and for life). A long time ago, a hockey ad appeared for skate manufacturer Bauer (now Nike/Bauer). The ad panned over a pristine sheet of ice and simply asked, "With a clean sheet of ice, what will you write?" Meaning: Endless possibilities await you when you're faced with a blank sheet of paper. Or a video camera. Or your life.

Without having conceived a product yet, you can focus on your passion and creativity. Plus, you can carve out your niche—whatever that niche might be—with no limits or walls (for some that is overwhelming; for others, it's exhilarating). And by carving out that niche, you can create your community—your participants, readers, viewers—before you need them or have something you would like them to purchase. Plus, as your content becomes more popular, you will have a tiny army (or militia) of people interested in you to help you with feedback and even offer suggestions for products they want to buy from you. These might end up being virtual products, real-life products you can hold in your hand, or services.

My grandpa used to tell me this all the time: There is a difference between a business and a hobby. A big question you have to ask yourself is HOW do you plan on monetizing? Can you afford to NOT make money right away and moonlight until you can?

That being said, you CAN start becoming a media source before you have a product. For example, Timothy Sykes took a similar approach: He began with his passion instead of a product. He now generates over *1.4 million dollars per year* through online content. Impressive, right? And it all started *without* anything to sell.

Fast–forward: Timothy still doesn't have a community of millions of people—a fact that disproves the misconception that is takes HUGE numbers to generate revenue. In fact, he has a community of about *2,000 people* that somehow make him more than 1.4 million dollars. Sounds pretty darn good, eh?

So, what the heck is going on here?

Well, Tim had a background in investing—including penny stocks, hedge funds, and some other finance-related passions. Therefore, his experience qualified him as a resource for others. He made—and lost—a lot of money in the market over the years, so he learned from that. Tim started writing and posting videos at www.timothysykes.com about his successes and failures in an attempt to help others invest wisely. He built up his community over time (more later about how to do that). Via simple polling, he started asking a few vocal members about the kinds of products they would like to see. He asked people if they wanted DVDs, a paid membership site, a special newsletter, personal consulting with him, and so on.

And that is how Tim developed and continues to create products. It wasn't rocket science, and it didn't require that a HUGE number of people be interested in his products. When he started out, he simply asked a couple of hundred people what they wanted. You can find a couple hundred people to provide you with ideas, can't you? Or how about 20?

And then there's 37signals: an iconic online brand for a software and technology company led by unconventional leaders Jason Fried and David Heinemeier Hansson. Their products, such as Basecamp (an online collaboration and productivity tool for keeping teams on task during projects) have an almost cult-like following—and have helped the company soar to millions in both subscribers and revenue. David and Jason also wrote *Rework* a highly recommended book about doing things (and by things—I mean entrepreneurship) differently. These brilliant guys also have an extremely (I mean *enormously*) popular blog called Signal vs. Noise. The blog, which boasts well over 100,000 subscribers, offers musings, articles, videos, and other tidbits on design, business, usability, the Web, and more.

However, Jason and David's popularity didn't happen overnight. Patience and persistence were the keys. During an interview with David, I posed a chicken-or-egg type question: What came first? The blog or the product? Honestly, I was expecting him to say the product and say something like, "We developed our first product and then thought, hey, let's blog!"

But it was just the opposite; the blog came first. And actually, it was a side project for the pair. They worked on building a community of like-minded people and then offering those people a product while keeping their likes, dislikes, and passions in mind. And they became thought leaders. Brilliant.

The lesson here is you can develop products over time and still start building your community *now*. It probably won't generate revenue right away, but it could be something you do at night (a little moonlighting) or as a side project. However—every streak starts with one. Every media source started with an idea and that first reader, viewer, or listener. The difference now is that creativity is more important than a big budget.

A Fluff-Free Story

I actually followed this path in my own career, by focusing on my passions for excitement, entrepreneurship, marketing and promoting, schmoozing with interesting people, technology, and innovation. More specifically, I embraced the idea that business doesn't have to be boring. However, I did so many unnecessarily complicated things at the beginning—such as hiring expensive production studios and more—that I came to realize: It really *is* true what they say about hindsight being so much clearer.

My initial idea for *The Rise To The Top* was a simple one (or at least, became simpler over time): Create a non-boring resource centered around a show (plus articles and other content) for like-minded, forward-thinking people. It was designed for entrepreneurs (current and aspiring) looking to build their businesses; marketers wanting to innovate; folks who were attempting to embrace technology. I wanted to interview the best, the brightest, and the most passionate—people with a great story and lessons to learn from. My revenue model started as sponsorships, partners, and events; I wasn't offering a tangible paid product to the community. In fact, I wasn't even sure what that product would be.

Finally, after two years of experimentation, listening, and pivoting, I found my product. I'm passionate about many things in my professional life, including video, talking, and learning from smart people. I love learning and sharing what I learn with others; it is that simple.

I'm also passionate about writing. One of my aspirations has always been to write a book. But not a half-assed book or one that I dictate to someone else. I wanted it to be something where I could get my hands dirty, pour in the maximum effort, and inspire others. I was waiting for that elusive "Ding!" moment where I could bridge:

1. My passion.
2. What my community (and others like them) wanted from me.

Realize that without combining both number one and number two, you (and really, anybody) are in trouble. Without number two, you create something you are passionate about but that nobody wants (oops); and without number one, you create something that's in demand but that you never truly get excited about it. Money follows passion—not the other way around.

One day right around Thanksgiving of 2009, I had a shockingly nonbusy afternoon. So I sat down and started writing an article on marketing predictions for 2010. I based it on personal experience; interviews, and conversations. As I wrote, I was in constant communication on Twitter, asking folks for ideas and suggestions for the article's title. Almost immediately, I began to receive tremendous amounts of feedback and inspiration. Sort of like having an advisory board made up of thousands of people.

(continued)

(*Continued*)

The title for the final product was "10 Big Marketing Predictions for 2010," and it was published on my website late that afternoon. As soon as I posted it, I received a quick note from a friend on Twitter saying, "Dude, this is the marketing article of the year."

Now, I'm certainly not claiming to have written an article that is the *ultimate* in entrepreneur or marketing education. (Yikes—that would be a jerk face thing to say.) But I was confident it was pretty solid (and I definitely don't feel that way about everything), so I shared it quickly via social networks and shot an e-mail to a few people with whom I thought it would particularly resonate.

And suddenly, the article—and more importantly, the ideas contained within it—started to spread.

One of the people whose attention it captured was none other than Guy Kawasaki—one of the biggest names in the entrepreneurial world. This cofounder of "the online magazine rack" (as he calls it), Alltop.com, and author of several best-selling books (including my favorite, *Reality Check*) shot this simple e-mail back to me.

Love it. Will tweet this 3 x.
Thanks,
Guy

So he linked to it on his blog and spread it to hundreds of thousands of folks on Twitter. And although the article was already spreading fairly quickly, Guy ensured that its popularity and momentum skyrocketed.

As a result, the article received over 30,000 views on my website in less than 48 hours. It was spread on Twitter over 750 times and received hundreds of comments. It hit the front page of some major websites including del.icio.us and popurls.com, somehow was reprinted in one of the top marketing magazines in China of all places—and perhaps most amazing, I received an e-mail from marketing legend (and personal hero of mine) Seth Godin, letting me know that *he enjoyed it.*

This inspired in me both confidence—*and* more ideas. At the bottom of the article, I asked folks what I should do with it—turn it into a video series? A framework for a book? E-book? The answer that came flooding in via e-mail, Twitter, Facebook, and comments was: "Write a book!"

And so, this article—"10 Big Marketing Predictions for 2010"—turned out to be part of the foundation or at least the spark for *Smarter, Faster, Cheaper.* And it all started with some free time I had on my hands one afternoon.

So why did I tell you this story?

It's not to brag about how awesome and brilliant I am. I know better, and by now you should, too. It's simply to provide a personal example that goes along with the thinking of Timothy Sykes and the gentlemen of 37signals: It is okay to start building and interacting with your community and trying out some creative approaches before you have a product.

5 | Be Your Own Media Source

Why be your own media source like the examples in the previous chapter? Because of the benefits it offers to your business, your brand, and to you, personally.

Is the time and energy spent created a multimedia source with you at the helm really worth it?

Without a doubt—and here's why.

Have Control over Creating Your Content

This is exciting. It's a big deal! No longer are you confined to *only* traditional means of marketing like pitching to journalists who may or may not be interested in writing a story about you. Or to TV producers who decide if your content fits their demographic. Or purchasing ads that are confined to 30-second spots, a limited amount of print, and other old-school mediums.

Now *you* are in the driver's seat. You don't need permission or to follow any particular rules. Sure, there are best practices (and really bad practices) you can learn more about—but

whatever you can write, shoot, or record is your media on
your terms.

Failure Is Part of the Game . . . and
It Has Never Been So Cheap

There isn't a road map for compelling content becoming a
media source.

For example, think of a laboratory in which a mad scientist
is at work, crafting his next invention. Now *you* get to be that
crazy scientist who tries a million things to see what works
and what doesn't. Contrast this with a failed campaign of the
past, wherein you would have to pay a PR firm all kinds of
money to beg for media exposure based on some kind of
angle for a story. And if it didn't work? Well, you were out a
ton of money—with nothing to show for it.

Or, you hired a fancy schmancy marketing agency that
recommends a radio campaign with explosions and talking
animals. It will only cost $25,000 to "try it out"—but then it
doesn't work, or you can't measure the results. That was an expensive mistake. And $25,000 could be $2,500 or $250,000 or
$2,500,000—depending on your business. That might be okay
for big companies but not for hustling entrepreneurs like us.

Now let's say that you yourself create a video or write an
article—without the fees associated with agencies and firms—
that doesn't receive very good feedback or response. Oh well.
The content police don't come and arrest you. And you can
try something else that day or tomorrow. What is your cost?
Simply your time and energy.

The barrier of entry to syndicate and get your content out
there online and onto mobile phones does not really exist. You
don't need to pitch a well-known magazine to get started.

And if you don't have an advertising budget to spread the word? No problem—even though there are some amazing, new, smarter, faster, cheaper ways to advertise coming up later! It used to be that you could spend millions just attempting to get SOMEONE to listen to you. Not anymore. Now you can let the world decide by making sure you get your content onto social networking sites like Facebook, Twitter, and LinkedIn and asking these users/followers/fans to let you know how they like it. You can network one-on-one with people who share the same passion and interests. You can form real relationships. Some great benefits include getting instant feedback and becoming a part of a cool community. REMEMBER—don't overly self-promote and end up being "that guy"; instead, focus on giving first.

There's Nothing Better than Free Opportunities

Posting to your website is free. Most social media sites are free to use.

Promoting your content and making connections *does* require an investment of time and creativity, and because the barrier of entry is so low, you have to be extra special to stick out. While this is amazing news on one level, it does mean that you have to be that much better. Or faster. Or more creative. Or more specific. Or unique (but hey, that is all part of running a remarkable business, right?).

Sharable and Spreadable

The best content is like peanut butter: easily spreadable. Word of mouth at its finest. The Internet has completely changed word of mouth by allowing one person to easily reach hundreds, thousands, or, in some rare cases, millions of people in a matter of seconds.

And people love to share. Especially if it is interesting. Or useful. Or really funny.

What kinds of information do people share?

The answer is simple: Content—all forms of it. Video. Articles. Photos. Lists. Advice. Stories. Artwork.

What do people NOT share? Ads and other boring, useless stuff. When was the last time you shared an ad? "Hey, Tommy, check out this really cool blinking banner ad! Wow!"

We have become a sharing society because of the tools at our disposal. And they are getting easier to use by the day.

Let's pretend that we're operating during pre-Internet days, and I wanted to share a newspaper article with my friend Jennifer. I would have to cut it out, put it in an envelope, and send it via Pony Express/the U.S. Postal Service. That takes *a lot* of time and effort. Think about all the dreary tools and supplies you need to make that happen—scissors, a pen, envelope, stamps . . . well, you get the idea. And there it goes, off like a herd of turtles to Jennifer.

Now imagine that Jennifer wanted to pass this article on to her friend Elizabeth. She would have to take the article (maybe copy it if she wanted to keep it) and repeat the above process. Elizabeth might decide it's not worth the trouble to mail the article to anyone else. So that's the end of sharing. A whopping three people read the article—the information in which probably wasn't even current or relevant anymore by the time the third person got her hands on it.

Nowadays, it is much easier to share good stuff. A click of the mouse. Cut and paste. Scan. Attach. Via social media, mobile phones, e-mail. All kinds of media—with more coming out all the time—sharing overload! And what is even more interesting about this is in many cases, sharing is taking place on very public forums . . . enabling it to be spread further.

That is why so many people are obsessed with retweeting on Twitter. When Twitter first was developed, retweeting (the ability to quickly pass on interesting content in public to your followers) was not a built-in feature. People just started doing it. And if you think about it, it makes sense. If you share something with me that I like, then I will like you for sending it to me. And that might lead me to check out your blog or website. And perhaps we will do business in the future. Who knows?

Bottom line: We like to share. People of all ages and demographics are sharing their thoughts, ideas, and great stuff from other sources. And it's fast, fast, fast!

Ease of sharing, however, means that your content has to be that much better—interesting, relevant, useful, and current—to rise to the top.

Search Engines Eat Content for Breakfast, Lunch, and Dinner

Our good friends the search engines *love* new and relevant content. Why? Because a search engine's goal is to match searchers with the best calculated guess as to what they are searching for.

Search engine optimization, or SEO, is one of those things that often becomes far more complicated than it truly is. A few geeks sort of mastered it in the past and didn't want to pass on the secret sauce to the rest of us. Well, here is the (really much simpler than you might think) deal with SEO.

Search engines like content that is new.

Search engines like content that is relevant.

Search engines like content that is linked to other sites (the better the other site, the more relevant the link is).

Additionally, there are all kinds of free data available as to exactly what people are searching for and how often. For example, if your product is website design for small companies, you find out what people are already searching for in your niche.

This paints a really pretty picture for creating content, because if your content is good (and free!), it will be linked to. Nobody will link to your About Me page. Or your product description page (unless your mom has a website and links to it). They just want the good stuff, the useful stuff—the information that countless other people want.

Online Content Can Increase in Value over Time

Bear with me here, as this is going to be a bit of a weird analogy: Online content is like a long-term relationship. And pre-Internet traditional media is like a one-night stand.

Confused yet?

Let's turn back the clock to that unthinkable time when the Internet didn't yet exist (I know—impossible to imagine). You (or your PR company) pitched and pitched your magic plunger product and finally got it on TV. Hooray! Lots of people see you, and some visit your store or call your toll-free number to buy your product. It is all quick. Fast. And then it is over. TV moves onto the next story. The long-term effects are minimal.

It was hot. It was sexy. It was gratifying at the time; then it was over. And if people missed it, they missed it.

Now fast-forward to present day.

Online content stays up—in most cases, forever, or until you choose to take it down. This means that even six months from now, someone can link to a post you put up today, last week, or last month. It also means that value can increase over time—just as it often does in a long-term relationship.

That video from six months ago? Perhaps someone discovers it today. And he becomes a fan of yours. And then he buys your product or service. Nice.

You can also leverage any traditional media exposure in this way. Most sources (radio, TV, newspaper) now put their content online so you can embed it right onto your site as well. A little extra content never hurt nor does the social validation that traditional media still confers. Your friends will be impressed—and so will potential clients and customers—that traditional media deemed you worthy of coverage.

I've found from personal experience that this is truer than ever nowadays; I'm always surprised when I see a hit on a post that was created months or, in some cases, years ago. I've had bloggers contact me MONTHS after something was posted to request an interview. The cost of keeping it up? Zero. The benefits? Potentially limitless.

How Creating Content Positions You as a Trusted Resource

Having expertise in an area is critical, and creating content positions you as the trusted resource in your industry when done correctly.

In short: *You* become the authority. When you are producing content, your status as a trusted resource on a topic
goes through the roof. Of course, you must continue to learn
more about your niche—something that could land you some
great coverage. For example, my friend Ria Sharon is a great
"mommy blogger" on her site mymommymanual.com. Her
blogging led her to secure a recent TV appearance where she
discussed new baby items that were just hitting the market.
Experts like Ria get quoted in the media (both traditional and
new). Trusted resources earn attention.

Contrast that kind of response with that which a traditional salesperson or marketer or business owner often
gets. People don't like those terms nearly as much when
it comes to trusting a person. Consider the saying, "People hate to be sold to but love to buy." By making the selling
process something different—entertaining, enlightening, and
fun—you put yourself *way* ahead of the game.

However—you have to *earn* it. No one becomes a trusted
resource overnight; it isn't a light switch that magically gets
turned on. You've got to work at it; become educated on a
topic; learn from current trusted resources in this book and
elsewhere; and do your research. (The key word here is "do.")
You can start right now. Get your expertise and knowledge
out there. Now is as perfect a time as any. If you are waiting
for permission, here it is: Go for it.

Take Dan Schawbel, for example. Still in his 20s, Dan
has become world renowned as a personal branding expert.
He has been featured all over the place (online and offline)
in such prominent publications and sources as Fox Business,
Forbes, the *New York Times*, and many others. Dan's Personal
Branding Blog is extremely popular; it has allowed him to
create his own mini media empire, which includes *Personal*

Branding Magazine, Personal Branding Awards, a book entitled *Me 2.0*—and he has even extended his brand to start Student Branding Blog. Now Dan offers consulting and other services as well.

When it comes to personal branding, it is safe to say Dan Schawbel is *everywhere*.

How did he do this? Simple: He decided to become the go-to person on this particular topic and worked his butt off. He didn't ask anyone for permission. Dan was employed when he started Personal Branding Blog. He did it as an after-work project, and it grew because he had the three elements of success: passion, personality, and knowledge. His knowledge came from his college experience of learning how to market himself, which was a great jumping off point. Obviously, his knowledge has only increased since that time; but it began with his own experience of working at seven different internships and learning how to pitch himself for jobs by sticking out. He then taught college kids, via blogging, how to do the same—and of course, he was speaking from experience. This evolved into a Personal Branding Blog where Dan posted interviews with the founders of well-known brands and wrote articles for other media sources to grow the brand. At that point, his empire began to take shape, and his expertise and influence continued to grow.

Traditional and New Media Love Trusted Resources

Pretend for a second that you are a reporter. Or a blogger. Or someone who books people for TV shows or who analyzes story pitches all day from people who think they are buzz-worthy. You are working on a story and you need an expert on wine. What would you do first?

Well, you might Google "wine expert" or something similar. Who comes up? Since Google loves content, there is a good chance that many of the results will be from someone who creates content about wine, not someone who is just a wine seller or pusher.

Or maybe you look through a series of pitches you have collected over time. One pitch is from Robert Pushman (made up name, I hope!) and the other is from aforementioned wine aficionado Gary Vaynerchuk.

Mr. Pushman talks about how he sells wine. And he probably rambles on about how much he knows because he does all of these wine tastings. Gary Vaynerchuk mentions he is the host of *Wine Library TV*, which has nearly 1,000 episodes (and growing) featuring him talking about wine for nearly 20 minutes each episode. And he is a fun guy to watch.

Which one of these men shines as the true expert on wine?

Realize that while both sell wine, only one focuses on expertise and content. The other focuses on the product. Content wins—every time. Thanks for playing.

There are also opportunities when it comes to being the local expert. Sure, the Internet allows you to be global without a passport, but something to keep in mind is your local town or city probably needs trusted resources for a variety of publications and shows. Think about the opportunities for you and your business if you became a regular guest or columnist. The publications definitely won't care about your product, but if you can prove your expertise, you have struck smarter, faster, cheaper marketing and promotional gold.

It's Not Just Online

Content is needed *everywhere*. Conferences are looking to bring in speakers. And conferences are definitely ignoring product pushers who want to come onto the stage and tell fairytales about how wonderful their product or service is. Companies want to hold educational seminars for their employees. Trade journals and magazines are searching for stories. This will be covered a bit more later—but always keep in mind that content isn't by any means limited to online. It simply spreads FASTER online.

There are plenty of offline means by which you can offer content to others. You can create seminars or host events that are focused around content and helping people. You can line up speaking engagements and other, less formal discussion sessions.

Yes, my friends, real life exists outside the online world. And smarter, faster, cheaper applies to online AND off.

The Cost of Creating Is Ridiculously Cheap

Want to create text? Here's what you need:
An idea.
A computer or access to one.
The Internet.
Somewhere to post it (your shiny, interactive website, for
    example).

Want to create audio? You need:
An idea.
A computer or access to one.

An inexpensive microphone and recording program to get
    started.
A simple program to edit the audio if you choose.
A space to post it on your shiny, interactive website.

Want to create video? You need:
An idea. (Are you noticing a theme here? You should be.)
A computer or access to one.
Some kind of camera (you don't need to be Steven Spiel-
    berg to be effective). It could be something you already
    have, like a webcam or a pocket camera. You can even
    use your cell phone (phone camera technology is get-
    ting better by the day). You can always scale up and get
    a fancier camera later—but for now, keep it simple.
A space to post it on your shiny, interactive website.

You can even do some editing, and you can keep it as basic
or get as fancy as you want. Some cameras have built-in editing software designed for everyone (not just the ultra geeky)
and/or a button to instantly publish to sites like YouTube or
your own video player. This is why it's always handy to have
our good friend the Internet around for these endeavors. It
provides countless possibilities for places to host your video
depending on what type you are creating in terms of content,
length, and so on.

Now imagine even just a few years ago how this would
have worked. You would have had to hire all kinds of expensive people and stuff to carefully craft your video. And where
would you publish it?

Nowadays, however, you have complete creative control.
And it's awesome. The level of expense is up to you. You
can always scale if you want to, maybe buy a fancier camera

or expand your staff. Or you might want to hire an outside consultant to help a bit. And many marketing and PR firms are innovating to assist with online content (and make sure YOUR expertise shines). But, the beauty is that you don't *have* to. It's all up to you.

Of course, new and different tools will pop up—some of which can change the game overnight. Perhaps it is an editing tool that allows you to edit with one click of the button or a new distribution method. Whatever new tools and toys emerge, whether you use them or not is your choice. But looking forward, the tools are becoming easier than ever. The opportunity to get started is right now.

Rookie mistake: Expecting an EXACT road map. When it comes down to it, who is the best source to learn from when you are taking the first steps to become your own media source?

Learning from successful people is often the key to getting a slight edge or spark. The funny thing is that those who do the best often don't have a road map to follow because everyone is different. You will, of course, do it your own unique way. Not their way.

Why learn from these trusted content creators at the top of the mountain? It might not work for you, after all—and that's fair enough. But the ideas and principles from those who've gone before you are useful lessons that you can use in your business. YOU pick and choose what is right for you. Entrepreneurs can learn from successful bloggers, new media sources, and innovative publishers. Why? They spotted this trend years ago. And they know how to build an audience. Though many of their business models (for example, sponsorships or advertising) might be different from yours, the foundations are similar—especially when it comes to creating and promoting engaging content. The difference might be as simple as their product differing from yours. But the best bloggers and new media sources have learned—and continue to learn—to market around their *product*. Whether that product is advertising, consulting, speaking, or a purple turtle figurine. Whatever. The point is you can make this personal. Most people may not want to become a Web celebrity. You might just want to attract a few new customers or clients. Or you might want to try and become as big as the folks at the top of the mountain. The same principles apply. How you use them is up to you.

6 | The Art and Science of Experimenting and Creating Content

Have you ever thought of yourself as a content producer? Are you a solid writer? Do you have a great speaking voice? Love to tell stories? Are you incredibly passionate about something?

The bottom line is that you—yes, *you*—can become a content producer, no matter what your experience level. There are usually four major reasons why folks do not take the content plunge: Fear, time, age/personality type, and obsession with perfection.

Fear

You might be afraid or apprehensive that the content you create won't be any good or that no one will listen/read/watch.

Perhaps you're afraid that you can't do it or won't understand the technology. I had that fear early on. I love technology, but I'm not a tech geek who knows all the ins and outs of it. So, I completely understand this fear. What I learned, though, is DO NOT let fear of technology hold you back. Sure, it might take some time to learn some of it, but it isn't nearly as complicated as you might think . . . and it continues to get easier. Fear of getting started is extremely common and completely understandable, but ask yourself: What is the worst thing that could happen? You put something out there, and you learned how to produce content. Hooray for learning! Not to mention, you now have a good story to tell.

On the other hand, imagine the best thing that could happen: that people DO like it—and YOU. After some hard work, you have a group of raving fans or community members who see you as an authority figure in your niche. Oh, and you make some money, too—either by selling your products or someone else's (with advertising).

Time

When am I going to find time to do this?!

How often do I have to update my content?

This is going to take FOREVER to produce.

These are some often-heard protests regarding building content—so consider each of these one at a time. Of course it takes time and dedication. Perhaps one less television rerun on TV (unless you are watching *The Rise To The Top*; in that case, keep watching!), getting up 30 to 40 minutes earlier or staying up 30 to 40 minutes later. Sure, you can spend hours on each blog post, podcast, or video—but pumping out quality content takes less time than you think with today's technology. You don't need a broadcast degree or journalism diploma or a massive TV network behind you to establish a following anymore. For those of you who seriously don't want to put the time in, becoming a content creator might not be for you. However, there are other ways you can benefit from online content (discussed later), including sponsoring content creators in your niche and some other goodies. And you will only increase in speed over time. Just like everything, it takes practice, and the first few times might be rough. Those who stick with it win the content game.

Age and Personality Type

The truth is neither one matters.

More introverted? Perhaps you are better suited for writing. More extroverted? Perhaps video and audio will be your thing then. The bottom line is that becoming an online content producer allows you to focus on your STRENGTHS! Nobody is telling you what to do, so go ahead and do what YOU are comfortable with. Old or young, there are no preconceived notions as to who can be a content producer. You don't have to be an outdated, overly-hair-sprayed newscaster to rock, or be like me and appear to be on your 20th cup of coffee 24/7.

Forget Perfection

So your grammar isn't perfect? You have a weird shadow in the background of your video blog? Audio drops on your podcast? Who cares? Just get the darn thing out there and tell your friends, colleagues, and anyone who will listen about it. Quality content mixed with great marketing is always going to be a winner. Get over whether you're supposed to use a semicolon or a colon.

The Internet is still the wild, wild West and the opportunity to stake your ground is plentiful. However, like many opportunities, your chances of seizing it are getting slimmer by the day. NOW is the time to become a content producer and claim your space. So don't worry about it if your dog walks in front of your camera when shooting (which, in fact, might be a good thing as it shows you are a human).

Finding Your Niche

Niche up my friends. While the traditional media world focuses on mass (and that is all well and good for them), the new media world is made up of specific niches. You can laser cut. For example, a show about dogs might do well on TV. A show about Cocker Spaniels may be too specific for TV but might work online. Finding that niche is so important online. What is yours? For example, the technology space online is really crowded. There are lots of technology bloggers, shows, and other stuff. There are big players who dominate the tech world like Robert Scoble (more on him in a bit). When Robert and I sat down for a chat, he mentioned how crowded the tech space is, but that it doesn't mean you should shy away from it if that is your thing. Instead, he suggested you simply have to get more specific and find what you are the best in the world at. From my experience, that is unbelievably true. Perhaps you could become THE resource on technology for moms or do a show on tech for people who are over 50.

Whatever. This was my thought when I started *The Rise To The Top*. My niche is young and young-at-heart entrepreneurs. That is definitely a space where there is competition. So, I had to differentiate. My differentiation factor came from the fact that many (not all by any means) shows about business, marketing, and entrepreneurship are super boring snoozefests or filled with so much fluff that you could literally create a bunny from scratch after each episode. That was the light bulb moment. I decided *The Rise To The Top* would be the non-boring, fluff-free resource and show for forward thinkers and that I could carve out that niche in a crowded space . . . I differentiated by just being me.

A perfect example of dominating a specific niche is Patti Stanger, known as The Millionaire Matchmaker. Patti has a booming matchmaking business and has a long-term reality TV show contract plus a radio show, among other things. She is a trusted resource, a personality, and an entrepreneur. When sitting in the offices where *The Millionaire Matchmaker* was filmed, I had the opportunity to talk to Patti about the keys to her success. Interestingly, Patti pulled the niche card. She talked about how the high-end dating market (millionaires and billionaires) was underserved (in fact, not served at all) as well as the men's market, and her expertise (being a third-generation matchmaker) enabled her to position herself as the expert in the niche. What niche can you dominate and become the thought leader in?

The Best Niches Have Similar Qualities

Passionate people: A subset of people who love the niche are passionate about it. Wine, animals, sports teams, whatever. And this passion might be indirect. For example, a lawyer could create an online show (video or audio) about avoiding legal mistakes with small businesses. You might not be passionate about the law, BUT if you are a small business owner, I'm sure you are passionate about small business. So, the show might be an excellent fit for you to watch.

Specific, but has longevity: What is something that should always be around for the most part? For example, cars will probably be around for a while. There is an opportunity there. Segways may not be around forever. A Segway as a niche is really specific, but it doesn't have longevity. They could be gone tomorrow.

Lots of material: Nothing is worse than a niche with a very limited amount of material. If you are in this for the long run, it has to be replicable. Think about why newscasts are successful. There is a format and there is always news. They won't run out of material . . . and even when they do (slow news days), they will find an interesting story about something.

Realize your niche may not be 100 percent in line with your product, but it must be 100 percent in line with your target community. You might sell coffee makers or consult with coffee lovers about who-knows-what (which would be weird, but anyway) and you realize your potential community is passionate about working virtually. There is the niche: Folks living a caffeinated, virtual working lifestyle. Boom.

So, let's say you want to jump into the content world and have the specific niche in mind. Fantastic. How do you take the plunge?

Similar to, well . . . every damn thing. Getting started has been overly complicated (shocking). In truth, there are really three ways you can get involved with online content—all involving a little bit of art. And these aren't mutually exclusive. Some people thrive with just one, while some find success with a mixture of two or all three. As with everything, it is up to you.

Create

Artists create. They come up with the material. So let's say you've got your own online channel. You write the content. You produce it. You promote it. This is the do-it-yourself model. And perhaps you find a trusted partner to help. Maybe you are really good at hosting but need some help marketing. Sounds like a good partnership opportunity. You can pick the hats you want to wear and outsource the rest ... while maintaining that ever-important authenticity. The one key piece of advice? Stick out. Try something different to stand out from the pack of content creators.

Become a Content DJ

DJs don't write the songs. They aren't artists themselves; they provide content on behalf of others. They curate. Select. Offer commentary. Show the very best. This is a great solution if you don't want to create your own content but want to be a curator (which doesn't mean you can't do this AND create content—sometimes it is great to mix it up). Becoming a content DJ means finding the best material and putting your unique spin on it: lists of best products/services, recommended books, hot articles in your niche, and so on. Guy Kawasaki does this every day with Alltop—what he calls an online magazine rack—where he brings together the top content for every topic on the Web. (A great resource AND example. Two birds with one stone here.) Alltop is a fantastic place to find good stuff to DJ in almost every niche. He also has a blog called Holy Kaw where he finds and shares things that interest him with a rabid audience. It just *works* for him. And it might work for you, too. Plus, you can still earn authority by being an active DJ—a DJ who makes sure his or her opinion is heard. Its akin to being a commentator on TV. Commentators don't write the news, but they do offer their opinions on it.

Sponsor Content

If being an artist isn't for you (or if you ARE an artist and are creating and want to juice up your marketing efforts), you can sponsor an artist and use the relationship to spread your products, services, and knowledge. If you don't want to do number one or number two but still want to get involved with online content because you see the vast benefits, there has never been a better time to become a sponsor of content creators in your niche. Why? Because even on the top blogs and online shows, it is still relatively inexpensive to become involved compared to all other forms of media (TV, radio, print), and content creators are extremely passionate and will make sure every dollar gets stretched, twisted, and maximized.

One of the best things about online content is you can break all kinds of traditional advertising and sponsorship rules for maximizing the relationship on both ends. I'm not talking about banner ads. I'm talking about feature-rich sponsorships such as guest blogging, an interview with you, branded content (which you can also put on your website), plugs, and more. Something that is spreadable, sharable, and longer lasting. A lot more about this in a bit (hold your horses—it has its own chapter!).

Find Your Voice

Text? Video? Audio? What is right for you? There are numerous examples of success with all the mediums and combinations. Some people prefer to create audio. Some video. Some text only. Some combine them all, while some swear by only one. There isn't a specific formula for success here—just two things you should take into consideration:

1. Your comfort level.
2. Your target demographics' preference.

Number 2 is interesting because the answer is really "everything"—as opposed to just video or just audio. For example, I don't think we could ever make generalizations such as "All tech-savvy moms prefer funny videos." I've polled literally thousands of people across different demographics, and their opinions are always split. And while there isn't a perfect medium, mixing them might be a great idea for your business.

Josh Shipp is one of the top youth speakers in the world and an extremely savvy entrepreneur who motivates teens (and parents). Although he looks about nine years old, Josh speaks TO youth (he isn't a youth himself . . . that clears that up). He's had massive success and absolutely dominates his market. And he creates a lot of content—including various articles and videos like his *Hey Josh!* series where he tackles key questions facing teens.

When I asked Josh what kind of content medium he preferred, he looked at me and said, "Assume half your audience is deaf. The other half is blind. If you are just doing one thing, you are missing out on [connecting with] 50 percent [of your audience]."

He makes a good point, huh? I'll leave it open ended. Would you rather appeal to 50 percent of your demographic using ONE medium you really love? Or would you want to spread it out and reach more?

The answer is up to you.

If you don't know, ask. If you don't have anyone to ask yet (we all started with zero), then experiment. See what works and what doesn't. Building a brand through online content takes blood, sweat, and tears. (Well, maybe not blood . . . then again, I *have* tripped over our cameras a few times. And walked into the occasional light.) However, the opportunities to rise to the top and the BIG long-term benefits are there for the taking for those who are passionate, have a vision, and stick with it.

The key is picking a starting point. Choose one to get rolling.

Consistency/Content

Consistency is huge. How often are you posting or planning to post? Do you disappear for weeks on end with no updates, and then create the ol' "Sorry I haven't posted in awhile!" post? While it's always okay to go on vacation or something like that (send me a postcard), why not give a quick heads up beforehand?

Think about the traditional media consistency model. TV, radio, print. There are seasons and schedules. Sure, we new media types play by our own rules—but consistency never goes out of style.

The really *cool* thing about new media (blogging, video blogging, podcasting, online magazines, content creating, whatever you want to call it) is that you can use different mediums on your channel. For example, it would be really hard for a TV show to suddenly focus on text the next day—awkward, and not really possible. But for you? *Completely* doable.

The Importance of Headlines

Imagine 100 articles are placed in front of you from 100 different authors. You are told you are allowed to click on just one. But, everything is anonymous with the exception of the headline. Which one do you click? The one that looks like a snooze? The most useful and functional? The most exciting? The most thought-provoking? The most emotion-filled one?

For one thing—and even though I wish they didn't—headlines matter. Is it complicated? Trying to be too clever? Too boring? There isn't an exact formula here; however, the shorter and more relevant they are, the more they get opened and shared. Think of it like one of those tabloid-terrible magazines: "Zombie Baby Eats Britney Spears!" It gets your attention, right? And attention has never been so scarce. As long as you have the quality content to back it up (we all know that terrible feeling we get about something we click on that promises to be one thing and is actually manipulative garbage), think about adding some spice.

Open Your Passionate Big Mouth

Life is way too short to be boring or not having fun. Is your content the life of the party or does it put people to sleep? Does it show your shining personality and unique perspective, or could anyone have written or created it?

This is the classic story of having fun: If you can have fun, you will enable others to do so. Think of it as having a squirt gun at the party, but instead of water, it is filled with delicious value. Sure, some buttoned up pleated pants folks might not like that you are having fun—but screw them.

Laughter and passion are contagious. Excitement spreads. Especially if you can help the reader/watcher/whatever-er. You might just have a new member of your community—or I dare say, a "fan."

Create an Unfair Advantage

I'm sure you have some kind of major advantage you can jump on. Don't be embarrassed by it; USE it. Go with it. Chances are that there's *something* that separates you from the pack.

Perhaps you are really, really ridiculously good looking like Derek Zoolander. Or super smart with a brain that others ogle over. Or maybe you're really outgoing or have a lot of connections.

Whatever your unique ability/characteristic/talent is, use it to your advantage. My unfair advantage (besides hair gel) was TV. I created something unique on television, which kick-started *RISE*. We began as a local TV show in St. Louis—first on My Network TV, and then Sunday mornings on ABC after (and then before) George Stephanopoulos and late night after *Jimmy Kimmel Live*.

TV was what I used to build credibility and separate myself from the pack, even though my ultimate goal was to create Web shows. How can *you* leave the others in your dust?

What about Scale?

Can you outsource content? Can you hire someone? Will it be too overwhelming?

Mashable is one of the top social media and web blogs in the world (remember, learning from geeky people is so important. They pave the way. And we are all a little bit geeky, right?). If you log on now, you will see a very professional setup. Lots of articles. Numerous contributors. Big-time advertisers and partners. While the real valuation of Mashable is unknown, it is estimated to be over 100 million dollars.

The takeaway here is scale. Mashable was started by the dapper Pete Cashmore in 2005—and he did it *all* himself. He wrote all the articles. He went to conferences. He reported. He generated interest. He tweeted. He Facebooked.

And then growth happened. It became too much for just Pete himself —so he started hiring folks. Editors. Journalists. Salespeople. And now Mashable has a lean staff that took them even further.

This may or may not happen to you.

You may eventually want to hire some journalists and content creators like Mashable or Hubspot, which employ their own staff of content machines (they are regular people, of course—not machines. But most of them create content like one). It's a fantastic option—as long as these people REALLY understand your company. The closer they are to the business, the better.

This is also a great opportunity for traditional journalists and you, the entrepreneur, to make a connection. We all know that there are a lot of out-of-work talented journalists—people who really know how to write. Or create video. Or host an audio show. Or . . . whatever.

Some are even more advanced—digital citizens who create (which is like the mecca of employees, if you can find them). These are folks who speak the rapidly changing Internet world lingo and know how to navigate it (and who probably wear cool jeans). If you can find a digital citizen who knows the Web world AND can create—well, you've hit a home run.

Take, for example, the website hosting company Rackspace. (I know, I know ... another tech example. Just because it is a tech company doesn't mean the lessons don't apply to you—even if you sell flowers, pet accessories, or consulting services.) While Rackspace certainly doesn't do the most riveting or sexy thing in the world, it clearly provides a useful service. After all, it is NOT a fun day when your website crashes if you go with the wrong company.

How does Rackspace market? Well, it has employed the Holy Grail of new age journalists and digital citizens: Robert Scoble.

Robert Scoble is a one-man (actually, two-man—since, as he pointed out to me during an interview, he has his cameraman with him) media source. He was one of the original bloggers at Microsoft back in the day and really did an amazing job of humanizing the company by interviewing people about the projects they worked on. Now, "The Scobleizer" is one of the top tech blogs online. Scoble breaks news, covers events, interviews people on the bleeding edge of the Internet—and is one of the most influential bloggers in the world.

Put yourself in Rackspace's shoes for a second. You need to get the word out about your service. You could take the typical approach ...

OR—you can hire someone who will become your own personal media marketing weapon.

What does Scoble do for Rackspace? He blogs in his own voice. He offers his opinions. But Rackspace powers his blog. "Powers" is sort of a cool term for "sponsors." There are displays and links as soft reminders to go check out Rackspace for hosting services. And occasionally he will mention Rackspace in his posts without being obnoxious.

So naturally, people click. It might be 1 in 10. Or 1 in 100; either way, they get there. Because they know and trust Robert.

The key here is that Rackspace knows that its potential clients and Robert's audience are a great fit. It knows that Scoble connects with web-savvy early adopters—and that is who the company is going after.

It's truly a match made in heaven.

Now, you might be thinking, "*Wait a minute, David. Didn't you say earlier that folks want to hear from the founders of the company or the folks in charge?*" I know, as an entrepreneur I love connecting to the top of companies. But, I believe the key is to connect with someone you know, like, and trust who demonstrates knowledge and is personable. Robert Scoble is the media arm and media source for Rackspace. The relationships he is forming are his. If tomorrow, another company nabs Robert, he takes his relationships with him. He is the personality, which causes a paradox for those looking to outsource: Are YOU the one who is going to be the face or are you going to have someone else do it? It is up to you, of course. But, there is a big difference between hiring a Robert Scoble (trusted and respected) vs. Joe the Actor (not trusted or respected). My opinion is to try it yourself first and then scale later if necessary.

7

Tapping into the Power of Online Video

Forget Viral, Focus on Function

If you are looking to educate, entertain, inspire, sell, market, introduce a product or service, add personality, and/or humanize your business—there may not be a better way to accomplish this than online video.

While nothing beats face-to-face real-world communication (I know—shocking, right?), the closest thing to it is video. And you wouldn't send an actor in your place when meeting with someone would you? Well, the same thing applies for video. The best voice is you (that whole authentic thing): the entrepreneur. The face.

Everyone wants to create a "viral" video. And sure, this is an insanely effective marketing weapon if you can do it correctly. But rather than trying to reach tens of millions of viewers, the real benefit of video to your business is providing content for a targeted market.

Think about this for a second: you can shoot video with an inexpensive camera and upload it for free for the world to see. And if not the world, at least your current and potential customers. Read that again.

Now take a pause.

I believe we have underestimated the power of what online video can do for your business.

It really is as easy as 1, 2, 3, 4, 5:

1. Camera (some ideas below)
2. The Internet + Distribution Method
3. An Idea
4. Promotional Strategy
5. Monetize and Measure

The price of video? Don't panic. It's way cheaper than you might think. No, you don't need a 20-person crew and a $15,000 camera.

And the best part is that everything that has to do with video is becoming less mind boggling. It seems like almost every day, a new, easier, more intuitive, cheaper solution pops up for shooting, editing, posting, and hosting (I think that rhymed). If you pay attention to trends, it is pretty obvious this is going to continue well into the future.

Sure, your videos have to be good; but they don't have to be masterpieces in order to be effective marketing weapons. And of course, a more expensive camera is going to produce better looking video than a cheaper one, but you can benefit regardless of your budget. The good news is that video can be used for almost ANY business, big or small (with a few regulatory issues, of course, for our good friends in the financial sector. But we still love you, financial sector . . . sort of).

Consumers are actually beginning to *expect* online video—especially since it gives your brand a face and a unique personality (can't hammer that point home often enough). There's no need for Spielberg-quality cinema, as long as expectations are set. For example: "Hey everyone, here are some underground videos." That one line will let people know not to expect a $1,000,000 production.

In his amazing book *Get Seen*—which dives into the easy technical details for shooting, editing, and getting your video online—author Steve Garfield covers the casual video revolution (I'd say Steve and I are using opposite sides of the brain . . . he is definitely the techie side). Steve explains that the rising popularity of videos is due to our ability to produce them inexpensively, simply, and casually; don't outthink yourself by writing a script for 100 hours and worrying about every tiny little shadow.

Take Jessica Kim from BabbaCo, for example. Jessica is a passionate entrepreneur who has a line of inspired baby products for savvy moms (the antithesis of moms who wear "mom jeans". . . you know what I'm talking about). Jessica is the epitome of smarter, faster, cheaper marketing. She grabs her camera and shoots little "webisodes" and videos that deliver constant advice for moms. It is simple and it works because, for one thing, Jessica is very real. You can tell she isn't acting. There isn't a script. It's just her, talking about her passion, and educating other mothers. Viewers feel as though they're actually in the room with Jessica, speaking directly with her.

She isn't pitching you; she is helping you. And you feel like you know her.

Before we jump into video's uses, ideas for your business, and what it can do for you, here's a brief technical lesson (cue documentary style music, please).

Smarter, Faster, Cheaper Hosting and Publishing

I can only imagine the complicated shenanigans that had to take place in the early days of online video (ask Steve Garfield, mentioned previously, one of the original video bloggers). The good news is that now, none of us has to worry about it—because it is so freakin' easy. Though YouTube wasn't the first site for online video, it quickly became the easiest to use. The folks at YouTube offered a simple means of posting online videos (and there are many sites now that offer a wide range of features and benefits). All you have to do is set up an account and you can upload a video for free. There are also paid options that work well as you get more serious, but really the costs are relatively minimal. That's it.

If you'd like some further ideas about this and other topics in this chapter, head over to my website, smarterfastercheaper.com, and check out some of the articles there.

Smarter, Faster, Cheaper Shooting

Hosting is one thing; shooting and editing were always a pain in the butt. And then this little David vs. Goliath company named Flip came along, and introduced a high-definition pocket camera called the Flip Mino. Close your eyes for a moment and picture a camera before the flip. I bet you are envisioning something BIG. Complicated. Lots of moving parts. If you were at an event and a cameraperson walked in with his really big equipment, you would stop and look at it. But the Flip succeeded by making HD video easy for everyone to shoot and edit. It has one button. It is under $200. It plugs right into your computer's USB drive. And it has its own editing software that allows you to do some simple editing and—with a single click—publish to YouTube or export to your computer. Wow.

Now, of course, the pocket camera trend is blazing hot; similar cameras and options are coming out constantly. Kodak introduced the Zi8, which took the Flip camera concept to the next level by allowing for an audio jack. iPhones and many other smart phones shoot fantastic video as well. And let's not forget our good friend the computer. Webcam quality is also drastically improving, both from internal webcams on Macs and PCs as well as some plug-and-play solutions.

It seems like everything is starting to shoot video. While no one knows what will appear next, it will almost certainly continue to build on the trend of simplicity.

Smarter, Faster, Cheaper Editing

It used to be that both on- and offline videos were ridiculously edited. Fancy graphics. "Quick cuts" (it was originally thought that people wouldn't pay attention for more than a few seconds before some kind of change in camera angle or graphic insertion or transition would need to take place). And it took a genius merely to figure out how to use editing software. Trust me; I tried some of them and wanted to cry a little bit. Nowadays, that has changed for two reasons:

1. **Consumer expectations**. Now that nearly everyone has watched an online video (even my grandma), it is safe to say that it is okay for video to *not* be heavily produced. If you want to, then go for it—but the real power comes from authenticity and message. And while this doesn't mean that your shaky hands will make you a cult favorite, it does highlight the benefits of being real and honest. Not everything HAS to be unscripted or improvised, but a little mess up here or there can actually be a good thing. People won't hate you; they'll relate to you. And the best part? You can always reshoot it. You might simply want to snip the beginning and end off—and there you have it.

2. **The software itself**. As I already mentioned, many cameras now come with built-in software. My Mac (yes, I'm a Mac fan, but I still have love for everyone) has iMovie, which makes video so simple to edit and export that I swear my mom's dogs could do it. And they aren't the sharpest tools in the shed, if you know what I mean. If you want to step up your editing game a little bit, there are some incredible Web-based editors that are as easy to use as point, click, edit—no physics degree required.

Great—so shooting, editing, and hosting have become smarter, faster, cheaper. But who cares unless it can do something for your business—right?

Think about this for a second: Video creates an incredible opportunity to market around the product (and not the product itself) and build your brand by generating interest. By talking about your passions and interests and helping others, you are well on the path to become a trusted resource. Interest leads to people liking (or even loving) you, and this leads to trust. And if people like and trust you, there is a much higher probability they are going to purchase from you—product, service, whatever. Plus, there are kinds of additional value, including creating conversations. Generating buzz. Attracting fans. Building community.

Why video? Let's run it through the smarter, faster, cheaper gauntlet.

Does it bring out passion and personality? (You didn't skip that chapter, did you?)

For one thing, video creates a great connection that is really hard to fake. I'll bet if I showed you two videos—one with a professional actor and one with a regular person—you would be able to spot who is who. It is really hard to fake video because it showcases your personality, passion, and knowledge.

And video has become extremely portable. Easy to view on multiple devices and mobile phones. It isn't tied to a computer.

Plus, video is really easy to turn into other forms of media. You can repurpose video to be text (a transcript) or audio. And, online video is still new, which creates a huge advantage in separating you from your competitors. Are they using video? How are they using it? Can you use it differently than they are? And, if they aren't using it at all, you've got an incredible opportunity to separate from the pack.

Are the eyeballs there? Yes. Beating a dead horse? I don't think so. More people are watching online video, and that trend is only going to continue into the future. Take YouTube, for example. While video goes WAY beyond YouTube, of course, this site provides a great example of the staggering numbers of online videos available today. YouTube is now the number two search engine on the Web, second only to Google, with over 70 million users per month . . . Wow.

In 2009, 80 percent of Internet users watched a video.

The eyeball shift continues. Video is becoming more sharable, spreadable, and interactive.

So let's say that you want your video to be passed along online. It positions you as the trusted resource. It lasts and can be archived and repurposed.

And because it is now smarter, faster, cheaper, you can AFFORD to experiment.

Number one video tip: Video falls in line with everything else related to online content: It can't all be about you. Seriously. The videos that generate the most interest are never the brag fests about how amazing you are (even though our mothers like to tell us so) or how great your product is. Instead, good video shares and amplifies a common passion and interest and/or focus.

Proven Video Ideas You Can Bring to Your Business

Tips and tricks: Education sells. Period. Brian Clark, from the famous blog Copyblogger, has made a living teaching others this principle (one of his programs is aptly named "Teaching Sells"). If you can educate folks around a passion or interest that's related to your product/service, then you provide a huge benefit and create a potential harem of people who like you and what you have to offer.

If you own a grocery store, why not film the butcher talking about prime cuts of meat or the best deals, giving advice for buying meats, and providing grilling tips? Or, if you are a speaker who talks about productivity, why not share a video series of your top productivity tips for folks? Or if you are selling software to lawyers, perhaps a video series on the top online mistakes that most lawyers make?

You get the idea. Ideas will spread exponentially if you put yourself in your demographics' shoes. What are they interested in? What gets them excited? Of course, this works in text and audio as well, but nothing creates a better connection than video (and you can intertwine all three for extra goodness).

And if you don't have something to sell yet, this is a great way to *build* a community *before* you create a product or service by allowing people to get to know you.

Shama Kabani has developed a reputation as a top online marketer. She has a successful Dallas-based marketing firm called The Marketing Zen Group and is the published author of *The Zen of Social Media Marketing* (a GREAT how-to book for social media). Shama markets to people who need help with online marketing and are interested in hiring her firm for services.

So how did Shama build her brand? Well, for one thing she practiced what she preached and became involved in social networks—and continues to be to this day. But she isn't just schmoozing and making connections (which, of course, is important as well). She also shares her videos from *Shama TV* and her weblog full of tips. When you watch the videos, you get to know her and her personality. Her dog Snoopy even makes a few guest appearances. And, in addition to being entertained, visitors always learn something.

Has this drummed up business for Shama? You better believe it! Her videos prompt people to want to find out more about her, and that leads to more and more people hiring her.

Realize that although she is giving away education here FOR FREE, she gets it back tenfold.

Even though it sounds counterintuitive, the more you can give away in content, the more of it people will purchase in the future.

Behind the Scenes

Giving customers a peek behind the curtain and letting them see how things are made can be really interesting in many industries. People love private access—especially if they can learn, be inspired, or be entertained by it. Why do you think backstage passes to concerts are so coveted?

This can work even if your industry isn't the most sexy and entertaining. People tend to be fascinated with what they can't see. How is your product made? Who are the people making it? What are their stories? Think about those random TV shows like *Dirty Jobs* and *Cupcake Wars*, as well as all the other documentaries and television shows that give you an inside view of a business. It is interesting for viewers and potential customers, and it builds the brand by creating more of that personal one-on-one connection by providing a peek into the process.

Product Demo/Screencast

Another internal video option that you can offer once you've gotten people to visit your site is to educate them on your product. This is a form of internal marketing. While a post like "Come watch our amazing product demo of awesomeness and amazingness" may not fly on social media sites or, heaven forbid, if you post it in someone else's blog comments or forums—it *is* enticing once someone is already at your site. Perhaps Google, or a brilliant piece of content you shared on Twitter, or an interview you linked on Facebook brought them there. Whatever your outposts are for bringing folks to your site, once you get them there, they can read/watch/listen to some valuable content (not a sales pitch)—something that will likely lead them to want to find out more about your product/service. Now is the opportunity for the product demo video (hooray).

This is your opportunity to show people why they should hire you and/or buy your product. It's a chance to talk about the problems your product solves and how it can improve their lives. The most successful videos talk directly to the potential buyer/client and answer the question: What is in it for them?

The key is to keep it authentic and not PR-driven or full of jargon. In many cases, you can walk through your product demo with a screencast of your computer screen. Entrepreneurial companies including Tungle.me (an online scheduling service) and TeuxDeux (an online to-do list) do a great job with the demos. They are short, to the point, and very real.

Storytelling and Online Shows

Another way to stand out online is to become better at story-telling. Think of the best storytellers you know. What makes them special?

Typically, they are:
- Likeable
- Trustworthy

- Captivating
- Humorous

And stories spread. They are personable. They demonstrate passion. They are *human*.

If you can tell stories that educate, entertain, and/or inspire, you will have a following—one that will lead to business.

Tim Ferriss (author of the highly acclaimed *The 4-Hour Workweek*) and Kevin Rose (founder of social bookmarking site Digg) are examples of two great storytellers. They are compelling, interesting, and great at speaking from their unique experiences. They don't try too hard. And they teamed up to create an online show, aptly named *Random*.

The show is shot simply, with just one camera, at random cafes and locations where Kevin and Tim just hang out and schmooze. They tell stories of travels, business, books, and more. They make observations. They offer their opinions.

And it works. It is captivating and fun, and provides great content. And I'll bet if you watch Kevin and Tim's show, you will grow to truly like them. They are entrepreneurs whose creativity and gift for gab really make them stand out. Are they pushing their own stuff on the show all the time? Not really. Does it help to build trust and authority? You bet it does.

Shows. There is an incredible opportunity right now to carve out your own niche show online. Having your own show is an unbelievably cool marketing weapon (even if it isn't done overtly). There are lots of options in terms of how you shoot, produce, and run your show. It is a ridiculously fun adventure that combines the use of creativity and technology all while building trust, likeability, and authority.

You might want to be the host of the show, or perhaps someone else within your organization is better suited. Perhaps the show focuses on interviewing or product reviews. Or advice.

The neat thing about online shows is that you can create multiple formats if you choose, including video and audio. People can watch directly or listen while in the gym, car, or while doing work at the computer.

For example, there is always tech news. Here are two creative entrepreneurs who are living examples of the best at tapping into this market. Both have their very own unique spin and product.

Leo Laporte comes from the traditional media world, having hosted a show called *Call for Help* on TechTV—his idea and baby. But the very station that gave him the opportunity to initially do it suddenly took it from him. So Leo decided to get over that disappointment and create his own online show: *This Week in Technology*. Although the show is really designed to be an audio-based podcast, he now offers a video feed (sort of like behind the scenes). Leo has gone incredibly big with this; he now has multiple shows and aspires to be the CNN of technology . . . online. And forget about catering to short attention spans; though Leo's shows range in length, they're often up to two hours long.

Leo was a comparably early player in the online content game, and he has benefited immensely from this. Early adopters (tech people) obviously started consuming online content before the rest of us (the ones who are still primitive, glued to just TVs). But a shift has occurred that's made this kind of media part of the mainstream; it doesn't just apply to technology any longer. There are now shows for a huge variety of demographics. Interior designers. Pet lovers. Home improvers. Sports card collectors. All shapes and sizes. And you can be successful even without a massive audience or community. The only show that is missing is *yours*.

Nowadays, Leo has multiple shows including some favorites such as *net@night*. He has cohosts, special guests, and a custom-made cottage he made where he creates all his content. He is always introducing or discussing something new.

And what is Leo's product? Well, it is advertising—and not traditional advertising. Leo does personal plugs for products he knows, likes, and trusts—and he only accepts ads from companies he knows, likes, trusts, and uses. You won't find Chico's Bail Bonds advertising on his show. It's an admirable methodology with great integrity.

Leo is doing quite well. Last year, his TWiT network brought in 1.5 million dollars in advertising revenue with only a few hundred thousand dollars in expenses. And revenue has nearly doubled every year over the past few years, while expenses remain low. I'd say that is smarter, faster, and *definitely* cheaper.

Do you have to go as big as Leo? Nope. But you might. And even if any of us do just a fraction of what he has done, we will have accomplished a lot.

Amber MacArthur is also in the technology area, but has a bit of a different model. Amber's show, *CommandN*, that she produces with her brother, Jeff, and friend Will Pate—features tech news, opinion, and more. It is quick-moving, with segments shot in different locations, and is normally in the 15- to 20-minute range with new shows released once a week. And while Amber does have a sponsor or two, the show's product is Amber herself and her media company, MGI Media. People who watch might be tempted to hire her as a speaker, buy her book *Power Friending*, or hire MGI Media to create their website. See how that works? The show is a smarter, faster, cheaper marketing weapon.

And shows may create new monetization opportunities and business models for you (hint: sponsorships and advertising). A little (or a lot) of extra cash is a good thing, right?

So what do the preceding examples teach us? For one thing, there is no single approach or one-size-fits-all road map. Within each niche, there is an opportunity to be innovative and share your unique voice, your spin, even your sub-niche.

My advice is to pick something replicable. Think of various talk show models—Oprah, Jay Leno, David Letterman, *The Daily Show*—where the premise is that there is always something to talk about. There are endless celebrities to interview and countless books to review. You get the idea.

Nothing is worse than choosing a topic or area of expertise that has a very limited amount of material. For example, if you were to interview every gourmet chef in Ames, Iowa, you would have very limited material (no offense to all the wonderful cooks in Ames, Iowa) and a very short show.

A Few Tips from Blood, Sweat, and Experience

Create something unique to stand out. This could be an unusual style or format. You don't have to go with the status quo. Pay attention to the kinds of videos that are already created and popular, but push yourself to be different.

You can't fake it. I was having lunch with a friend of mine when suddenly he stopped and said, "You know what I love about video? Unlike text and other forms of media, you can't fake it." I thought about this for a second and it is SO true. Be honest. Be you. Otherwise, we will see it in your eyes.

Order of importance. 1. Content (Content is king. No joke.) 2. Audio (Nothing is worse than cheap sounding audio.) 3. Lighting 4. Video Quality

Add in text. Search engines love text, and you, in turn, should love search engines—because they help people find you. Try having an accompanying article or a transcript if you insert video of any kind. If you have video posted on YouTube or another video sharing site, make sure to fill out the detailed paragraph describing your video.

Play to your strengths. This goes along with being yourself. If you are funny, aim for funny. If you are a straight shooter, use that approach. Just go with it, and be authentic. Not sure what you are? Experiment and see what comes naturally to you. You can always ask some friends for their honest opinions.

Don't force consumption. You know those annoying videos that automatically play on some websites? Don't do that (unless you want lots of upset people looking for the stop button and then clicking away forever). Let people CHOOSE to watch your video or listen to the audio. Put it in a prominent place, of course—but steer clear of the ol' auto play.

Grow bigger ears. I'm not just talking about getting ear enhancement surgery here (ummm . . . does that exist?) I'm talking about likes and dislikes. What else do your potential fans/customers watch? How do you acquire this information (short of stalking them)? Tap into the power of social media. Facebook and Twitter are big digital footprints. As your audience/community builds, ASK THEM.

Patience. Whether you are just looking to make a couple of new connections or wanting to build a video empire, it takes more than one month and a single video. In fact, it takes MANY months and MANY videos—along with persistence, resilience, and experimentation. If your content is good, it will rise to the top over time (hey—what a great name for a show!). More on how to actually attract those eyeballs in the next chapter.

Perhaps you will start a video blog with tips and tricks. Or interviews (discussed next). Or behind-the-scenes looks at things you've learned. Or funny videos. Or a show of some kind that combines everything.

Video is only limited by your creativity, which you have a lot of, right?

So give it a shot. Try it out. Don't overthink it; just see if you can make video work for you and your business. If you can, you'll be amazed at the results.

8

Market and Promote Your Business by Helping Others

Interviews are an amazing way to build your brand; this has been my primary winning strategy with building *The Rise To The Top*. However, I'm FAR from being the only one to find success by using this method—and this is definitely not a case of "this is what I do, so you need to do it, too." Interviews are platinum. They're valuable—very valuable.

People love to be inspired and entertained about subjects they enjoy. For example, let's say you love hamsters. If a pet food company decides to do a series where they interview dancing hamsters, there is a good possibility you will tune in. In turn, you just might become interested in the hamster food brand (that whole thing about companies and brands as media sources and publishers). And this is true of every niche. Interviews with passionate people are instant brand and credibility builders. Plus, they're easy to promote, and you get the added bonus of learning something and forming new relationships.

Interviews create the ultimate triangle of awesomeness. The interviewee wins because they get to be in front of your community. Your community wins because they receive valuable content and information. You win because you are promoting others, providing great content, and generating interest.

So, how should you conduct an interview? They can, of course, take place in person—but another way you can do it (and eliminate geographical challenges) is to interview people online. With webcams becoming all the more common, all that you and your interview subject need is a computer, webcam, the Internet, and some simple communication software like Skype. Or, of course, you can just record the audio.

Skype isn't the only way to do it; however, I've learned from personal experience that it works really, really well. I know this all sounds a bit overwhelming—but don't be nervous. I'm not suggesting that we all need to be like a late-night chat host and perfect interviewer. But chances are that you'll draw more people in—and garner more customer interest—by broadcasting conversations with others.

So, who do you interview and how do you land it?

Thought leaders. Every niche has thought leaders; it doesn't matter if you run a funeral home or sell flowers. There are the trusted resources in every field, and the Internet has made many of them all the more accessible (which is amazing). The benefits of interviewing thought leaders and interesting people in your niche are vast. And doing so builds your credibility, since you will be associated with these people. (After all, if you were a serial killer or con artist, these people probably wouldn't allow you to interview them.) Having these conversations builds trust.

Another major key here is the unbelievable promotional opportunity this provides. It is so easy to promote other people. And more often than not, your interviewees will also promote the exchange via their channels—something that is instantly amazing, regardless of whether they have a following of 25 or 2,500,000. It is sort of an unwritten rule in interview land that if someone interviews you, you will help promote him or her in some fashion (on Twitter, Facebook, e-mail list, whatever). Give first, and you will receive.

Up-and-comers. A little bit of research in your niche will reveal those rising stars. People who might not have a massive following but who do have great ideas and are interesting. Perhaps there is a new blogger offering some great insight. Or someone with a new product that just came out and who is hustling for coverage. Up-and-comers are amazing interviews. Why? Because they are superpassionate and really care. I'm not saying big influencers don't care—they certainly do—but those looking to make it really have that hustle and drive. If you help them out, only good things will happen. Even if your audience is just a few people, you are helping. And that is big. Plus, up-and-comers will really promote the heck out of you. They need to get their name out there and will most likely promote the interview by doing everything short of tattooing your website on their chests.

Your interviewees also reap benefits by granting you these interviews regardless of how big your audience or community is. Perhaps they have something to promote so there is a value to them being interviewed by you. Many will share it with their communities. Perhaps they will send out a tweet about it. Or a Facebook update. Or an e-mail. Or blog about it. Or a pigeon messenger (well . . . maybe not that one). These interviews are long lasting, spreadable, and sharable; they're easy to pass on, and they stay up forever (unless you take them down), which follows some of the key benefits of online content.

Don't be afraid to ask for interviews. While it can be intimidating at first, you should realize that leaders are people, too. And inviting them to chat on your website assists them as well, because they get to connect with your audience (regardless of how big it is). It is the ultimate win-win.

A short, to the point, and specific approach is the way to land interviews. Plus, do some research for goodness sakes. Most people you would want to interview have some kind of online media source (blog, website, and so on), and often they will let you know the best way to contact them. Some people love e-mail. Some hate it. Some will only respond on Twitter . . . in public. It varies. E-mail is often the best route, though, if you can't discover a preference.

Mixergy.com founder Andrew Warner interviews successful tech entrepreneurs (we are in similar, exciting niches with different models and personalities).

Andrew shares the template he uses to land interviews.

The three-part layout I use:
Line 1: A single sentence that clearly asks for what I want.
Line 2: A sentence or two explaining what I do and what this interview is about.
Line 3: A link to a past interview so they can see a sample of my work.

A sample of the e-mail:
Hi Seth Godin:
Can I interview you via video Skype on Tuesday, Sept 1 @ 11 A.M. Pacific?

This is for Mixergy.com, where I interview entrepreneurs about how they launch and grow their businesses. I'd like to interview you about how you built Squidoo.com.

You can see a sample of my work in this interview with (insert unique person here).

I will occasionally throw out a couple of dates when I contact potential interviewees—but never too many. It's a fine line. Plus, you can build up the level of people you approach over time. You can't expect to interview someone at the very top of the mountain right away (even though you might be lucky enough for this to happen). It took me a LONG TIME before I interviewed Seth Godin on *RISE*—and it was well worth the wait. Start smaller by tapping into your existing network.

Another way to land interviews (which takes a little more sweat but is worth it) is to meet folks in person—at conferences, for example. Some of the most inaccessible people suddenly become accessible when speaking at an event. Sounds like a great opportunity for networking and to land guests.

One thing I've noticed is that video interviews are great for busy people you want to interview— and who isn't busy, really? A text interview means they have to type out the answers, which takes a lot more time than turning on the computer, heading to Skype, and answering a few questions. While this is also the case for audio, a video automatically comes with audio—so people can listen or watch, and you can get it transcribed to text as well. Three birds (video, audio, text) with one stone (video).

A tip: try to catch people you want to interview when they have something going on they are trying to promote—a new product, service, book, event, and so forth. Even the most successful, hardest-to-reach people suddenly become much more accessible when they are introducing or producing something new that they want others to know about.

How you conduct the interviews is really up to you and your personality. You might be the no-nonsense type, or you might take a more chatty approach; whatever works. Or perhaps "10 Questions with (insert cool guest)." The goal is always to make your subject look as amazing as possible. Your audience will let you know what they like over time. The key is trying various methods and seeing what is a good fit for you and your business.

Your Customers

Interviews aren't limited to big-time thought leaders by any means. You can also interview your current customers and clients to ask about their experience honestly (not like those late-night infomercial mock discussions). While this may not be something you overtly externally promote ("Hey, come watch our customers talk!"), these are great for internal marketing, promotion, and proof to offer for visitors to your website. Plus, there is no better endorser for your business than other people who have actually purchased something, or subscribed, or used your service. And if they have big mouths, they will probably tell other people—which is always a good thing.

37signals—a company I mentioned earlier in the book—does this all the time. Upon visiting its site, you'll see the interviews the company has done with a whole slew of customers—from an independent art retailer to an attorney. As a consumer, you'll most likely relate to one of these people—because 37signals picked out diverse and ideal customers to interview. Lawyers will relate to the lawyers, accountants to the accountants, and so on with a whole range of other service professionals. It's actually a pretty brilliant methodology.

Bottom line is you don't have to be a professional interviewer to get and give value from interviews. It might be the big idea that propels your brand to the next level.

9 | The Keys to Marketing, Promoting, and Building Your Community

In the business world, if you can't market it, promote it, and leverage it, you might as well not do it. That is the fluff-free reality of it. You can have the world's greatest product. You can be the world's greatest person. You could be an absolute all-star at creating content. But, if it doesn't spread and reach the right people, you will have a cold glass of no sales mixed with a shot of irrelevance.

A big misconception is you create something incredible and everyone comes beating down your door with money, fame, and glory. Does this happen? Maybe once in a zillion times.

Rookie Mistakes: Zero Patience and Wasting Time

Although I've emphasized the importance of smarter, faster, and cheaper (as opposed to dumber, slower, expensive), don't confuse "faster" with "instantaneous." At the end of the day, all of this takes time. Very, very few people watched *Wine Library TV* for the first eight months when Gary Vaynerchuk initially launched it. My first blog posts got about nine views. Eight of those views were my dad. Jason Cohen, founder of Smart Bear Software and author of the A Smart Bear blog, told me in an interview that he started blogging, and blogging, and blogging . . . a lot of time passed . . . and then after several years it became popular.

Realize that a community and audience isn't built overnight. It evolves and grows over time. But the time you spend will be worth it.

If you are impatient like me, this is tough to swallow. No sugarcoating here. It takes effort, time, drive, and passion. Comments won't come flooding in right away. The money train won't immediately make a stop at your home. Ravenous, passionate fans won't be stalking you at your local coffee shop (yet). If you really believe in what you are doing, you can move forward and enjoy the slow burn and be truly happy with what you are doing and creating. One post at a time. One person at a time. This process is definitely a passion tester. If you don't have it, someone else will outwork you.

One trick I learned at the beginning was a bit on the mental side of the game based on confidence. You have to be confident that what you are putting out is fantastic and will help people. Second, I tricked myself into thinking that I had a big community before I had one. I (internally) pretended I did. It was a little mental trick that kept up my confidence and drive. I would think to myself, "I must get this post up today or 100,000 people will be pissed!" Now it is 100,000; back then, it was just a few. But it kept me on track day-by-day. And I bet it can help you, too.

I know some people might point out here that this goes against the "faster" principle (yeah, yeah. I know I promote that idea). But faster really *does* apply here—because you can *create* faster. You can talk with people faster by using a simple click of the mouse and keyboard. You can reach people one-on-one faster. This is really a dream situation for any business owner and marketer.

And your speed will increase over time. Think about back in the day when you learned how to read. You got faster with practice.

Your time—and any given person's time—is finite. The biggest pitfall here is to spend all of it creating—worrying about this word or that word, staring for hours at a shadow in your video, being concerned that it is not perfect, and other endless time wasters. None of us is Shakespeare or Spielberg. This doesn't mean that we should rush through the creation process and put out garbage. But from my experience, and picking others' brains, you have to focus at least as much time and energy on marketing and promoting (hence, this section of the book).

Those who have created strong content often skyrocketed because of the 20/80 rule. Twenty percent of your time is allotted to creation; 80 percent to promotion, relationship-building, and so forth. This isn't meant to be a scary fact or an encouragement to put out subpar content—it's simply the reality of it. As opposed to worrying for one hour about the grammar associated with one word, your time is probably better spent doing other things: schmoozing on social media, commenting on other websites in your niche, and utilizing many more strategies we are about to discuss. Over time, this might change if you get huge (if that is your goal), but marketing and promoting will always be important. That is why you often see up-and-comers taking on the giants. The giants can lose their hunger.

Can you get away with less? Maybe. But, nothing replaces good old-fashioned hard work and getting your hands dirty. If you want it badly enough and you have the passion, personality, and knowledge . . . you can do this.

So, how do you spread the word and build a community of passionate people? When it comes to building a community by being smarter, faster, cheaper, and promoting and marketing the heck out of your content, the components are:

- Creating a sharable and spreadable website.
- Expanding your network: schmoozing, networking, and interacting.
- Reputation and participation.
- Building better blogger and new media relations.
- Using your content as a handshake to connect with anyone you want.
- Smarter, faster, cheaper advertising and sponsorships (traditional advertising is SO YESTERDAY).
- Taking it offline.

While the tactics vary, there are key smarter, cheaper components to building your community. Feel free to blend, mix, and use as you will. Some will scream your name; some might not resonate with you at all.

Not All Web Traffic Is Created Equal

If you break it down simply, there are several ways someone can discover you and your amazing content and website.

One-to-One and One-to-Many

Word-of-mouth online and offline. Perhaps your dad bragged to someone at the grocery store about your website. Or your business colleague told someone at an event. Or one of your fans shoots an e-mail to some friends or tweets about you. Someone passes on your content via Facebook. Whatever.

Your Social Media Accounts

Your followers and friends. People who are connected to you in the first degree.

Search Engines

Building authority with search engines takes time and great, relevant content. There are a few ways people can find you via search. The easiest, of course, is they hear about you from some OTHER source and enter your name or company name. Great. Realize though, those folks have to have had some kind of other clue from another source leading to this point to know to enter your name or company name (or they are REALLY good guessers and, in that case, should be on a game show). Over time, your content is how people discover you on search engines. Doing a Web show on ponies? Perhaps one of the shows is titled "Tips for Purchasing a Pony," and when people search for "purchasing a pony," they find you.

Advertising and Sponsorships

Someone saw your ad online and offline and made the trek to your website.

Yummy Links

I bet if you could eat a link, it would be delicious. Links are huge—especially when coming from reputable sites. This could be everything from a blogger mentioning your awesomeness to a guest article you wrote to someone submitting one of your links to a bookmarking site.

Places Where You Participate and Leave Your Footprint

Perhaps you regularly comment on other blogs in your niche that offer a link back to your website and/or forums where people are discussing whatever your passion is and you have your website in your signature. Every time you post and leave something insightful (and not sketchy), someone might click back to you.

Traditional Media Mentions

Super Amazing Magazine mentioned you? Nice. Hopefully some folks come check you out and the magazine was also nice enough to link to you on its website.

Other Random Ways

A link in your e-mail signature, a mention in a book, and who-knows-what else can also bring the people to you.

Some of these ways cost money. Some cost time and effort. Some are hard to monitor and measure. Others are super easy. Some you have complete control over and with others you have zero control. *Not all traffic is, of course, created equal.* Would you rather have 3 people discover you and become super fans or 1,000 find you, take one look, and go away? Finding the right mix that works for you, your personality, your style, and your budget is part of the fun. (Remember that non-boring thing? This should be fun. Hooray.)

Wait a second—what is all this talk about building a community?

For many people in the traditional marketing and business world, the concept of building a community is foreign. But not to you, of course.

Traditional thinking dictates that the only goal of marketing and promoting is to attract customers. But a community does so much more for you than an individual customer ever could. A community spreads your content and products. A community refers you to others, builds loyalty, and wants to help you as much as you help it. A community is made up of real people, not random numbers.

Audience versus Community

A community is *not* an audience. An audience passively listens, watches, or reads. A community interacts, questions, challenges.

An audience is one-way, not interactive or social. An audience doesn't participate or share with others.

A community, on the other hand, is a two-way conversation—a living, breathing *thing*. Extremely interactive. Social. Sure, some people just watch or read, but many also participate and share with their friends. This isn't to say an audience isn't important. It is. There will always be people who just want to consume your content and get on with their day and that is fine. Both an audience and community are important. There is no way around it: Creating, maintaining, and growing a community is tough work. But if you are passionate and patient, the rewards are huge and lasting.

The following chapters discuss strategies that have been key to building up our *RISE* community as well as drawing on conversations with some of the top bloggers, new media sources, and innovative entrepreneurs in the world.

10 Creating a Sharable and Spreadable Website

If you think about it, your website is your house. You can have the best marketing and promotion in the world, but if your house is a mess, nobody will want to come over or come back.

The corporate-speak, one-way website is dead (or at least near death and digging its own grave). It has always been boring, but now it is really on its way to the marketing museum of old ideas.

Your website is your first big impression. It is your home that you invite others to visit. Actually, some get invitations, and some just show up at your door, unannounced. But both kinds of guests are great.

Have you ever met someone who is sharply dressed? He talks eloquently. He probably has some great stories to tell. He is modern, hip, and fun. And then he invites you over and to your absolute shock, his house is stuck in 1972. There is gold shag carpeting. There are *Brady Bunch* posters. It is like taking a trip back in time. Does your impression of him change? Would you trust him? Would you want to find out more?

What about the online equivalent?

Your online house is a reflection of *you*—your personality, style, and ability. It needs to be welcoming, interesting, and comfortable—a great place to hang out. It needs to compel visitors to want to stop by again and again.

Let's say you are meandering through Facebook or Twitter, reading the comments on someone's blog, or just Googlin' around. You notice something interesting that someone else has said or posted, so you click and head off to their website for the first time.

(This scenario is the same regardless of where you hear about the website—social media, Google, in real life, other forms of marketing and advertising—God forbid, a billboard or on the side of a bus.)

And then you get to this website—and it is terrible. The design is messy and unprofessional. Some links don't work. The last piece of updated content says April 2, 2003, and you can't find the information you are looking for. There is no personality. No pizzazz. It isn't inspiring. It's a snooze and a huge letdown.

What happens to your opinion of that person and her company after encountering such a disappointing setup? Do you trust her ? Do you want to do business with her? Or do you want to click away and cry yourself to sleep (a little dramatic—but you get the point). I know I click away, never to return.

If your website is not well-designed, simple to use, and clearly expresses how it can help people, you will lose potential customers/clients/fans in *the blink of an eye*. It doesn't matter if you have great ideas and an outstanding product; no one wants to hang around long enough to find out more about it. It's like having a lumpy sofa and no TV. Who's going to kick back and relax at *that* house? They'll move on to a more exciting neighborhood with better homes.

Let's say that you create 20 videos on YouTube that get thousands of views. Then, out of the blue, Google suddenly announces that YouTube is being shut down tomorrow. However unlikely a scenario that is, if you don't have a home base, your brand could disappear from the Web overnight. Tools will come and go. Having an updated, modern, easy-to-use website positions you for the long haul.

Consumer expectations for your website have evolved in pretty much every industry. Customers expect more over time, and what is new today quickly becomes commonplace tomorrow.

Times change and expectations change—and your website needs to change with them.

What do consumers expect nowadays? First and foremost, simplicity. If there is too much confusion, people will go away. It's sort of like going to the supermarket and finding 87 different kinds of toothpaste. It causes confusion. There is a trend right now to throw every bell and whistle onto a website and what you end up with is a pretty mess. Nobody likes a pretty mess.

Plus, in this era of the social Web, there is this incredible opportunity to be more human, interactive, social. Sure, your advertising agency charged you exorbitant rates for that fancy flash intro and those cool graphics. But are people buying

from you? Can they give feedback? Can they easily connect with you on social media sites if they choose to? Is
there a COMPELLING reason I should sign up for your
e-mail list?

If your website is sitting on the top of a remote mountain and you're using a bullhorn to blare to your potential
customers down below—then who's going to stick around to
listen to you flap your gums?

And that's where a well-designed blog comes into the
picture—one that encourages comments and publishes your
shiny content. Your platform.

If the mere word "blog" makes you think of little kids in
skinny jeans, replace it with whatever makes you feel better.
Here are few alternative names.

- Channel (your own TV channel)
- Show
- Video blog (or vlog)
- Online magazine
- Monkey house (okay . . . that one may not work)

It is where you place the content you make.

As long as you easily update content by constantly providing new entries and allow for interaction in the form of comments, e-mails to you—whatever you like—then it constitutes
a blog. And the best part? An extremely well-designed blog
that's optimized for search engines and easy-to-use-even—for
the least technical amongst us—costs a tiny fraction of a full-
fledged outdated website.

And here is more good news. Creating an unbelievably
cool, custom-made website *used* to cost an arm and a leg, at the

very least. Ten thousand dollars would have been considered cheap—and the price tags for many professional websites had multiple zeros added on. Now? You can get a really nice, social and interactive website under your full control for FAR less.

Now *that* is smarter, faster, and cheaper.

If designed well, optimized for search engines, and full of interesting content (as well as helping customers solve a problem), you have a recipe for a successful website.

A website is more than just a few pages about your company. It is a platform, a hub to spread your ideas and a colossal marketing asset.

Remember to use your real estate wisely.

Things to consider in addition to content

- What is the FIRST thing I want people to do when they come to my website?
- Is it easy to SHARE and SPREAD the material I post? Can users e-mail it? Tweet it? Facebook it? How easy is it to do this? Can it be done with just one click or a maximum of two? (This is *incredibly* important.) The other HUGE component is adding the right plug-ins to your blog to enable this sharing (for the nontechies, think of a really nerdy voice explaining: a plug-in is simply a very small program you install into your blog/website). If you have to put on a safari coat and go hunt for the button to send it to Facebook, people won't do it. Make it easy to send to the most popular sites at the very least.
- Is it clear to users how they can contact me? Do I tell them what the best way to reach me is? E-mail? Phone? Twitter? (Make sure to specify, as people differ

in the ways in which they're most comfortable communicating.)

- Are you tastefully tooting your own horn? Are media
  mentions, blogger mentions, and so forth all linked up?
  How about a list of some of your best customers and
  clients? Social proof is something that should not be underestimated. Social proof says to people visiting your
  website, "I'm good enough to be covered and contribute to some media sources and here are some customers and clients who trust me. I'm good enough for
  you, too!" You will come off like a big deal without
  being a jerk. Nice.

- Can people visit my website and then easily find me on
  social networks if they choose?

- How do I keep people coming back? Can people subscribe via e-mail for updates by using RSS? (RSS stands
  for Really Simple Syndication, which, in a nutshell,
  is a massive online reader where people can subscribe
  to multiple blogs and sift through them on one easy-
  to-read screen. It's sort of like subscribing only to the
  TV channels of your choice, if you could. Or channel
  surfing on demand to access both new and old stuff.)

- Is the important stuff above the fold? (The fold is exactly
  what it sounds like: the middle of the screen. According
  to Neil Patel from KISSmetrics (a big-time entrepreneur
  obsessed with websites, data, and the online hustle),
  eyeballs naturally stick around the top half of websites.
  Is all of your important information in that general area?

- Are there calls to action to purchase something? Or take
  the next step in some shape or form? Is it easy to find
  out more about your products and services?

Creating Your Ideal House

Establishing your hub is just as important as the marketing strategy and promotion tactics you use—and your website's design is a critical feature. Sure, there are free (and cheap) templates out there; however, I would argue—based on both personal experience and thousands of conversations that I've had with others—that it is worth it to hire a strong Web designer and developer to upgrade your site. Or, at the very least, buy a great customizable theme that you can make your own (sort of like buying the inner workings of a car and then having someone else work on the aesthetics like the paint). This should still be smarter, faster, and cheaper than the old school arm-and-leg prices and method for creating a site.

There are all kinds of blogging services that are amazing and free (which is incredible, if you think about it). And while those services can be a strong base for your site, I'd highly recommend differentiating, stepping outside of the template box, and adding your own personality.

Show your passion. Make it your own.

First Impressions

What happens when people start comparing websites? If clients and customers are browsing between you and competitors—which many are—then you'd better believe that your design matters. Think about the last time you compared companies (all things being equal, meaning you simply stumbled upon them, or two people you trust equally recommended two different companies). Would the simply, dynamically designed site win your trust and business—as opposed to the site from 1998 with a little cartoon construction guy digging?

We entrepreneurs know that both online and offline media can provide huge opportunities to grow your business. When journalists come to your website (and inevitably spend a SPLIT SECOND there), do they see something that is easy to navigate? Or do they see a mess?

Good design allows you to separate yourself from the pack, which is ALWAYS a good thing.

After all, fitting in is *so* high school.

The Two-Brained Website

If you think about it, a smarter, faster, cheaper entrepreneurial website really has two functions: content and product.

The content portion is everything mentioned above. The stuff you create: videos, audio, photos, articles, whatever. Plus, all that fun, interactive stuff such as subscriptions, links to stalking . . . I mean, finding you on social media sites, comments, and the rest of it.

The product side is the next step. The point of purchase. Where people go to learn more about your product, contact you, download a trial version, watch a video, read testimonials, or actually *purchase* something.

Whatever those next steps are.

But the two-brained website isn't like a mullet (party in the back and business in the front). In other words, there doesn't have to be some massive disconnect between the content and product in terms of design or personality.

Imagine that you are hiring a clown for a child's birthday party (just go with me here) and the clown agrees to meet you beforehand. He shows up and does some of his best tricks for you—making balloon animals, squirting from a flower on his shirt, and performing other favorite stunts. You love it. So you tell him you are thinking of hiring him. The clown tells you to hold on a second now for the business portion of the conversation—and says he will be right back. He then returns, perfectly groomed and wearing a designer suit. No clown hair. No makeup. He has a stern expression and a briefcase. He places a list of testimonials in front of you. Then a rate sheet.

What would you feel? A massive disconnect, perhaps?

A divided website that differs in personality, message, and tone is just like the clown, before and after. It is akin to doing the same business with two completely different people.

This isn't to say your website is actually two different ones. It might be. Perhaps one is www.youramazingshowwith anengagingnamebutnotaslongasthis.com and the other one is www.youramazingproduct.com and you simply link between the two. But, an even stronger play is to have one hub that proudly showcases content first.

Internal Marketing on Your Website

Before jumping into promoting your content, let's talk a little bit about internal marketing, meaning making your content work for you.

So you've created this amazing, personality-filled material. Someone comes to your site to watch, look, listen, and/or read. Awesome. High-five!

But, that doesn't generate much in the bank, does it (unless you have an advertising/sponsorship-based model)? Are you reminding your potential customers that you have a product for sale without forcing their mouths open and shoving it down their esophaguses ... esophagi? (Does anyone know the plural of esophagus?)

Remember: Your number one goal is to be a trusted resource, *not* a product pusher. Once you have established your expertise in an area, you want to approach the product- or service-selling almost as a friendly reminder. And there are many ways to gently remind people about what you offer.

You can put links in the bottom of your posts, or add cues to your site's navigation bar. As you earn credibility and trust, you can add in a promotional post now and then. You can mention your product briefly at the end of videos, or tastefully pitch it at the end of webinars or e-books.

The rookie mistake here—which many have made—is to use your content as a trap to sell something. Customers can smell this a mile away. So be upfront and honest.

A Fluff-Free Story

My experience with websites has been QUITE the adventure—one from which I hope you can learn as I have (without making the same expensive mistakes I did).

My first entrepreneurial endeavor was an inline hockey league (I know, weird) that needed a website. Although I know zero about programming, I tried to create the site myself (this was before all of the cool do-it-yourself tools were really mainstream). I built it quickly with iWeb for the Mac, and plopped it up there. It probably wasn't the world's *worst* website, but it certainly was not in the top 20 (zillion).

The problem with my handmade site was that the design sucked. It was extremely unprofessional. There wasn't any pizzazz or personality, and I was just guessing as to what people wanted. Plus, I didn't even know about analytics so I didn't measure traffic (yet another rookie mistake).

What happened next was this: I was approached by an expensive media company that informed me my website was lousy. And of course, they offered to create a good one for me—for around $15,000. I somehow scraped the money together and, like an idiot, hired the media company to build a new website. The new site was better, but I *definitely* overpaid.

After moving on from the inline hockey world to my true passion, The Rise To The Top, I took a very different approach to the website. Sort of like Goldilocks when she chose her preferred bed; I looked for the just the right mix between the do-it-yourself and expensive media company. I met Elizabeth Erickson, a very talented entrepreneurial graphic designer, and she introduced me to Nick Leidenfrost, a very talented Web developer.

It was a match made in heaven for many reasons. First, I learned that very few Web developers are excellent Web designers, and very few Web designers are excellent Web developers (two different sides of the brain, I suppose).

(continued)

(*Continued*)

I worked closely with Elizabeth and Nick, and we were able to bring my vision for my company to life. And I became a website nut during the process—visiting every website under the sun, learning about usability, analytics, and all that important jazz.

The lesson here is to really find a trusted partner to help you build or rebuild your site. Doing it yourself, unless you know design extremely well, might be more heartache than it is worth.

11 | Expanding Your Network

The Art of Digital Schmoozing

Digital schmoozing: my favorite phrase. Call it networking, relationship building, whatever you want. The bottom line is that your ability to network online and form real relationships is being smarter, faster, cheaper. And please don't confuse schmoozing with being fake—because that doesn't work online *or* off.

If you are creating online content and looking to build a community, you have to get active on social media in your niche. Share both others' and your own content. Ask and answer questions. Connect with relevant people. Listen.

It isn't rocket science; it is human nature. Your community is made up of humans, not robots. The more one-to-one connections you make—and the more people to whom you offer value—the better off you'll be. A simple way to think of this is an ongoing 24/7 dialogue. A dialogue that mixes sharing interesting content, small talk, and more. It doesn't mean you need to be monitoring social media sites 24/7, but it does mean that the more effort you put in, the more results you will get out.

So is networking also marketing? You better believe it is. Being able to market yourself and your business in the digital world is one of the most overlooked aspects of effective marketing. Relationship building, expanding your network, and marketing and promoting go hand-in-hand-in hand. This isn't a revolutionary concept by any means—yet somehow, many people are, well, pretty bad at it. Why?

Simple. While the principles of online and offline networking are extremely similar, the online world is a bit of a different animal.

Many people have mastered—or are trying to master—the tools (some as basic as e-mail, going all the way to Twitter, Facebook, and so on). However, mastering the tools and leveraging online etiquette and an understanding of the digital world are two different things. Social networking isn't like buying a billboard ad or having your cat be your alias. It is about making the one-to-one connections that goes all the way back to the way mom-and-pop stores flourished. At the end of the day, this isn't about the technology; it is about *people*. The world keeps getting smaller and more connected. Will you be able to adapt and market knowing that, in most cases, you can connect to almost anyone you want to with just a little bit of effort?

An online presence doesn't work for entrepreneurs if we aren't growing our network AND maintaining existing relationships. The social Web has created an incredible opportunity for two-way conversations with a click of the mouse or a video Skype call. We all know that. And it's *worth* the effort.

If you want to maximize the online world, you have to be online. *YOU*. Not your intern. Not your friend who wants to help you out. Not someone you're paying to do it for you.

And being social online doesn't mean cruising Craigslist for a deal on patio furniture. You are online to connect with well-chosen people—people who are interested in what you have to say (and you are interested in what they have to say)—and to share your passions and interests.

So where are these people? Are they watching online shows? Are they active on social media? Are they reading blogs? Are they high-tech, low-tech, medium-tech?

The one thing you know for sure is that they are definitely online. So get off Craigslist, stop downloading tunes, and find them.

The Dumber, Slower, Expensive Approach to Digital Schmoozing

The dumber, slower, expensive approach to schmoozing is nonexistent, contrived, or pushy-push. Nonexistent, of course, meaning zero focus on one-to-one relationships. Contrived meaning automated or "having the intern do social media." Not organic. Finally, pushy-push is the person ALWAYS trying to sell something and promoting his product and trying to manipulate you until you buy. Yuck. And it's all really not even very human. It is all about taking and not about giving. It is about pushing your message on others, without giving them a chance to react or respond.

True schmoozing is not about running campaigns. It's about connecting to and forming lasting relationships with humans and, yes, also advancing business interests (let's be honest here).

Scott Stratten said it best in his book, *Unmarketing: Stop Marketing. Start Engaging:* "You wouldn't send a mannequin to a networking event, would you?"

The dumber, slower, expensive approach meant trying to build a "list" as fast as possible. E-mail addresses. Twitter followers. Facebook friends. And what do you do with that list? You SPAM them, of course! (Really? You spam them? That sounds awful! Of course, I'm just kidding.)

The Goliath approach to digital schmoozing is often contrived. Forced. Measured. Robotic. And *slow*—given the corporate mentality of creating a board, thinking about it, forming a focus committee, spending money, coming up with big policies, and then finally (maybe) starting. The problem is that there is a lot of bad advice out there when it comes to social media. People or brands that already had a big following before social media existed in the form it does today could talk about the last adventure they had taking a shower and get a response. Good for them, but what about the hustling entrepreneur? We need to play by our own set of rules. Forget the big brands. Forget the celebrities. Let them play by their rules while we do it smarter, faster, cheaper.

The Smarter, Faster, Cheaper Method of Schmoozing

There are a lot of things in the modern business world that you can automate and outsource—relationships aren't one of them.

Relationship building happens by giving. Being social. Engaging in digital handshakes. Bringing the relationships offline as well. Indulging in small talk. Caring. *A lot*. Connecting people to one another. Educating. Inspiring. Making people laugh. Sharing high quality content—both yours and others'.

The results? You become the go-to person. People know you. They seek you out because they respect what you have to say and enjoy how you say it. And yes, people will buy your product. But that comes last!

It's All about the People

Imagine you love coffee (for many of us, this is very easy to imagine). And you attend the Coffee Lover's Conference. Over three days of meeting and mingling with the caffeinated crazy people, you literally shake the hands or rub elbows or awkwardly hug 100 people. Wow—that's a lot.

Of the 100 you met, you remember 20 really well—yet you're stuck with everyone's business cards.

When you get home, you connect with those 20 people and stay in really close contact with a few. Every so often, you will still hear from 1 of the 20, and only *very* occasionally, from some of the other 80 people.

By using this approach, you are expanding your network by being smart and not going for pure numbers. As long as you continue to offer value (perhaps you have a coffee blog, or share supersecret coffee drink recipes), you become someone valuable—not just a blip on the radar screen. You become an indispensable, trusted resource.

The pure numbers approach is the opposite. You meet 100 people at the Coffee Lovers' Conference. You take a half-assed approach to following up with all 100 by adding them all to your social media sites. You spam them with e-mail blasts (bad idea!). And you end up with zero real relationships, but 100 new virtual friends and followers.

Now, let's pretend that Twitter is sold tomorrow. It is gone. Goodbye. It's sort of like leasing office space in a building that's suddenly sold—and everyone is kicked out. In short—you are forced to go somewhere else.

And then, the next day, Flitter pops up. It is the new Twitter! Except all your followers and connections from Twitter are gone. You have to start from scratch.

I personally would rather have the real relationships. Because if people genuinely know me, and I know them—and we share a passion—I will find them, and they will find me on the next hot site that emerges. People you get to know online, maybe one day you meet offline (or not). People you meet offline then stay in touch online.

Real relationships trump any technology. Technology is merely a device by which we're able to stay in contact with one another; it isn't what business is all about. As long as you are active on the sites that YOU enjoy and YOUR NICHE is present in (and perhaps pick up a few schmoozing tips), you will have success. You will get out what you put in.

Imagine that tomorrow brings the biggest Internet crash of all time. Every relationship on every network is gone. You have to start again online. Who is valuable to you? To whom are *you* valuable? What people are just taking up space? Put yourself in another's shoes: Does that individual see you as a connector? A source of valuable information? A passionate, fun person? Or are you an expendable product pusher?

The Power of Being an Online Connector, Value-Giver, and Digital Schmoozer

Lewis Howes is a generous person. On any given day, you're likely to spot him online, helping people understand LinkedIn (as the co-author of *LinkedWorking* and a LinkedIn specialist). Lewis connects people. He introduces them on Facebook, Twitter, and LinkedIn. He blogs. He holds webinars. He creates content. He is generous with his time and talent.

In fact, I can trace a huge handful (a "huge handful"? Really? Is there even such a thing?) of people I know—and with whom I have great relationships—back to Lewis. Lewis initially contacted me several years ago. He informed me that he was coming to St. Louis to host a networking event and wanted to offer me a free sponsorship. He just gave me value right away—which demonstrated the basic principle of understanding the wants and needs of the person to whom you are talking. We ended up meeting up in person before the event and hit it off immediately.

Ever since then, we have been great friends. We have had speaking engagements together. We have introduced each other to key people. We share each other's content with our communities. And both our businesses have grown as a result.

I can trace some interesting events back to Lewis. Lewis introduced me online to Ria Sharon from MyMommyMan-ual.com, and she and I quickly became friends. One night, Ria held an event at an art gallery, which I attended, and Ria introduced me to the owner, Scott Scully. Scott happened to be an *über*entrepreneur with a marketing firm, sales company, and more. I invited Scott to be on my show to tell his story and help entrepreneurs. His appearance got a great response, and we continued our relationship. Now, Scott's company sells sponsorships for *The Rise To The Top*, and his company is also a sponsor itself. We continue to help him get new clients and he helps us. Now, I know that he has my back and I have his. And it can all be traced back to one message on LinkedIn. Crazy, right?

Lewis is what I would call an expert digital schmoozer. The interesting thing, though, is that Lewis was not really well known before social media. He followed the smarter, faster, cheaper guidelines (before they were written down in this handy book). The neat thing about this is that you can have success like him and many of the other examples in the book. You don't need to be superhuman. You don't need to be a big brand with big bucks. You don't have to have a previous celebrity status to build a following. The social media world, when you cut through the fluff, is really made up of two things: content and people. If you are sharing the right content and interacting and helping the right people, you have a formula for success.

Characteristics of the Most Successful Entrepreneurs on Social Media

First and foremost, they do a few things consistently and well, things that you can do, too. There is no degree or certification in schmoozing (a PhD in schmoozing, perhaps?). These are all things you can start doing right now.

The Best Online Schmoozers:
Are selectively present. I know, Captain Obvious here . . . you have to be present and show up at the party. In this case, the party means the different social

media sites. Sites like Twitter, Facebook, LinkedIn, whatever-the-hot-site of the moment is (remember the sites will change over time, but the ability and importance of connecting one-on-one with people online isn't going anywhere). But, the best don't attend every party (there are literally thousands of public and private social networking sites out there). They attend the right parties. The ones where they feel comfortable, and, more importantly, the ones where people they want to connect with in their niche are. For example, I love Twitter. It fits my personality because it is chatty and filled with quick bits of information—plus, many marketers and entrepreneurs are on there. So, I spend a lot of time on it, and it has been huge for building relationships and my business as more people find out about my show. While Lewis is very active on Twitter, he spends more time on LinkedIn. That is his bread and butter. Finding your bread and butter is part of the experimental process, but just remember you don't need the whole loaf. Instead, a better approach might be to do a few sites well. The bottom line is that *you* get to choose—based on your comfort level, and, of course, where your niche hangs out online—and what works best for you.

Show their faces. Yup, I know; it seems shockingly simple. But you can see who the best schmoozers are, and they aren't faceless logos; they are people. People want to know, connect, and ultimately do business with other *people*—not products or logos. Let the big brands showcase their logos. You get the fun opportunity to be a human. When is the last time you had a quality relationship with a logo? Did a logo ever buy something from you? Did you ever invite a logo over for dinner?

Share valuable content. This could be links to high-quality content in their niche. Perhaps it is useful, funny, or especially meaningful. In most cases, the content comes from two sources: you, the entrepreneur, and others. This means that it's your material; your Web show; your insightful, helpful blog post; your contest or event. The stuff you create—whatever it might be—combined with material from others, most of whom are thought leaders and up-and-comers in your niche—the big guns and the smaller guns. You can't be afraid to open your mouth and share your content on social media sites. After all, you are helping others with your content, right? Dan Schawbel (Personal Branding Blog, discussed earlier in Chapter 5) does this extremely well. He consistently shares interesting links involving personal branding and adds a couple of words to them. Dan is promoting others and his own links all while continuing to brand himself as a trusted resource.

Promote others more than themselves. Sure, you can promote, but do so for others first. There may not be an exact ratio, but a good rule of thumb is to endorse others more than yourself. And that doesn't just mean promoting their content; it means recommending other people, introducing people to one another, and helping people make connections. This works—because when you promote others, you create a reason to interact with them. And promoting others is just good business. Top blogger, social media thought leader, and co-author of *Trust Agents* Chris Brogan does this with the best of them. Take one look at Chris' Twitter stream or Facebook account and you will see him constantly promoting other people. Helping friends. Passing along "neat" stuff, as he says. Sure, he also promotes his own stuff, but Chris isn't a product pusher, he is a trusted resource. He lives and breathes the role.

Are helpful on their own websites and on social media sites. Helpful means answering questions. This is caring at its very core. When someone leaves a comment on your site, you have two choices: respond or not. It is up to you. Some people never respond. Some people respond to every comment they get, no matter what the topic.

Of course, over time, it will be difficult to respond to everything as your community grows. However, I've noticed that success follows when you make it a priority to interact with your community. Give every comment a hug—because someone took a bit of time out of his busy schedule to leave it.

The same goes for social media. Are you a robot or a person? If someone asks you a question, do you respond? How about if someone asks a question about flowers and you are a flower expert? Sounds like a good opportunity to jump into the conversation and interact. Now, of course, there are limitations to this. You can't sit there all day and answer questions or say hi to everyone; however, I bet we can all block out a little time to do so, can't we? Small talk and caring go a long way. Plus, it has never been so public. And you can't fake it or outsource it.

You can't fake caring. You have to commit to it. It's thanking people who do nice things for you. Asking people how their day is going (and listening to/caring about the answer). Offering to help. Being a good person. All of this goes a long, long way.

Are consistent. The best ones are always around. Sure, sometimes they aren't (it *is okay* to take a vacation once in awhile ... c'mon now). But, they don't disappear without reason (or a heads up). They work at it. They invest time and effort. They provide information on a regular basis. Their followers/fans/customers know that they can depend on them for this. Does consistency take time and effort? Of course it does. Consistency is a slow burn connecting to people one at a time. Being there. Meeting new people. Helping. One person turns into two. Two turns into three and the list goes on.

Have something to promote ... and do it tastefully. Social media isn't ALL about giving. It is about giving first, but the very best users who get the most out of social media professionally and personally have something to promote. However, in many cases just like everything else in the book, it isn't the product. It is their own content. A show or a blog. A webinar. An event. A workshop. Something valuable for others. Or it might be content created by others that mentions the entrepreneur or something that individual sponsored. Yes, you can toot your own horn. A lot of social media gurus sit there and say, "you have to listen, listen, listen..." but forget to mention you ALSO have to pipe up. Tweet about your new show. Tell the world about the interview you just did. Just make it about them and you will win every time.

Are masters of small talk. In an episode of NBC's hit television show *The Office*, branch manager Michael Scott and his boss Jan go to Chili's to try and sell paper to a client and end up landing a major contract. Jan tries to take the corporate approach by talking facts and figures. No personality. Boring. Big yawn. Michael, on the other hand, finds common interest with the prospect (played by Tim Meadows). They have some cocktails. They talk about marriage. They bond. And while Jan is horrified over Michael's behavior, he is the one who ends up closing the deal.

In this case, Jan is the no-fun naysayer who wants everything to revolve around results, ROI, campaigns, and professionalism. Michael approaches the client in an entirely different manner; he has fun, finds commonalities, chitchats, and forms a real relationship. And guess what? The deal still gets done. The results were still there.

Small talk is severely underrated. It is how relationships are formed. Small talk is engaging. Small talk leads to conversation and likeability. And small talk shows that you are human and not some kind of machine. You obviously don't want to forget about business; but for goodness sakes, be a human first.

What does this have to do with social media schmoozing? A lot. It isn't just about sharing links. It isn't (really ever) about what you had for breakfast. Asking people how they are doing, how their week is going, and thanking people goes a long way. Give it a shot.

Introduce and vamoose. Neil Patel is a hugely successful Internet entrepreneur and just a straight-up hustler (that is a good thing). He is an influential blogger and has built several hugely successful companies: KISS-metrics and Crazy Egg. Before he was 21, he was already named one of the top influencers on the Web. Neil obviously does a lot well, but one thing that particularly impressed me is his ability to be a connector. He consistently introduces people to one another that he feels should know each other. And then he backs off and watches the magic happen. He might introduce two people on Twitter. Or at an event. Or via e-mail. There are many options. What happens is Neil becomes the relationship source and a catalyst. Simply put, people remember people who introduce them to interesting people. Connectors are trusted resources. Can you make introducing a part of your routine?

Take the relationship further. The best schmoozers bridge and grow their networking online *and* off. They get away from the computers and attend events (many often speak at events as well). They bring people together, perhaps at their OWN events. (Do you put on your own events to bring like-minded people together offline?) They meet people everywhere and connect with them later on social media sites. Instead of a stack of business cards, they collect real connections that form a network. And this works both ways: meeting people you met online in real life and meeting people in real life and using online tools to stay in touch and maintain the relationship.

For example, I once posted information on Twitter telling my followers that I was in San Francisco at the Giants vs. Cardinals game (go Cardinals!). Someone from Twitter, whom I only knew online, replied and said she was at the game as well. We ended up meeting up, and now we've become business associates. From pixels to people—it really does make a difference. Amber Mac (one of my favorite examples of a smarter, faster, cheaper entrepreneur and previously mentioned) often tells the story of sitting in an airport and meeting someone because of an online connection. If you are open to expanding your network, good things happen.

Plus, there is an opportunity here to mix mediums even further. Perhaps you connect to someone on Facebook. They send you a message and then you initiate a phone conversation. Or meet for coffee. Or send an e-mail. Becoming a channel shifter and taking the relationship further is a key element of schmoozing that anyone can do.

Aren't afraid to expand their networks. The top folks aren't afraid to reach out to new people and extend a virtual handshake. And they aren't sending one of those "I would like to add you to my professional network on LinkedIn" generic messages. Instead, they are specific and tell people why they are connecting. For example:

"Hi (insert important person). Love your (article, post, show, Mom, face) on (insert actual subject). My name is (insert name) and I (insert what you do: your blog, show, whatever). Just wanted to reach out and introduce myself.

I doubt anyone will punch you in the virtual face if you do that.

Grow bigger eyes. It is pretty darn easy to find out who is influential in your niche. Perhaps they keep coming up on Twitter. Or they are a top blogger. Or you Googled around and found them. Not only do the top schmoozers connect with these people (more on how to do this in a second), but they also connect with people who follow and are connected to them. For example, if you are looking to connect to people who love cupcakes, there is a good chance the people who follow "TheCupcakeWarlord" on Twitter (made up . . . I hope) probably love cupcakes as well. Why not extend a handshake to a few of his or her followers? Perhaps share some cupcake recipes? Invite them to a cupcake lovers' event? Offer some kind of value?

Schmooze randomly. Interestingly, I've found this to be very true. Top schmoozers connect with and interact with people way outside their niches as well. In many cases, the most random people can result in very solid relationships. If you are a beauty consultant, it doesn't mean you can't connect with a football blogger. In fact, sometimes the best relationships have something else in common besides the niche. And you never know when people will refer you (and you them). I noticed this to be the case when I first started signing sponsorships for *RISE*. I never made a cold call. I never stood on the street waving a sign. I simply asked for a little help from people I had relationships with who I respected and had met *somehow*. Online or offline. I wasn't selling these folks anything, I was simply asking for a little help and a referral. Because I had a previous relationship with them (one way or another), they helped. I was given a name here and an e-mail address there and even some warm introductions. My random network had become a HUGE referral source, and I bet yours can, too.

Rookie Mistakes

What Not to Do (aka How to Shrink Your Network)

Follow Bad Models

There is lots of bad advice and terrible models out there. Some of the most established, visible people were visible BEFORE social media and play by their own rules (for example, Britney Spears). Let them. Who cares? But a word of caution: Do not emulate them. Britney Spears may be munching on a cheeseburger and telling us about it, but that doesn't mean you need to tell everyone about it when you do the same.

Share Irrelevant Details

I'm sure that every mundane detail of your personal and business life is riveting. I know how fascinating it is that you are eating a banana (post one); oh, and now you finished it (post two). You know the kind of people I'm referring to—the ones who post every little damn detail about their boring lives. Perhaps nobody has told them we don't care ... and perhaps someone *should*.

Brag All the Time

Accomplishments should be celebrated. You won third place at the Dairy Farmers Cow Milking Contest? Sweet. Seriously, that's great. But there's a fine line between being excited about something you've achieved and continuing to talk about all the amazing things you are doing without an end in sight. A far better approach is to recognize and praise OTHERS for their accomplishments or at least find a way that your accomplishments can teach others something. This is part of building a reputation as a generous business owner who is not threatened by other peoples' success and does not spend all day bragging about his own. What sounds best to you?

"I just won third place at the Dairy Farmers Cow Milking Contest!"

"My good friend Mike just won third place at the Dairy Farmers Cow Milking Contest. Go Mike!"

"Lessons learned from taking third place at the Dairy Farmers Cow Milking Contest."

I know I'd rather go with the second one (promoting a friend) or the third (making it bigger than just me). What do you think?

Forget to Talk Shop

While it's important to make small talk and occasionally joke around (if that fits your personality), the best don't forget about business, either. Every entrepreneur has something to sell, market, and promote. Make sure people know what you do and what you create. Are you sharing your content?

Spend All Day on There

Yes, social media takes time. Yes, it is super important. No, you don't need to spend your entire life on there. Staying behind the computer and tweeting or whatever-ing all day is not an effective long-term strategy. While you do get out what you put in, it is easy to spin out of control. Ask yourself: Is what I am doing right now moving my business forward in some way? If it isn't, get the heck off there and do something that does.

Being Overly Formal

Dear loyal *Smarter, Faster, Cheaper* reader: It is with warmest regards that I compose this literary paragraph. It is an absolute pleasure to connect with you on various social networking sites (as the kids are calling it these days)! I look forward to sharing a glass of brandy with you next time you visit my multimillion-dollar estate full of rich wood.

Sincerely and forever,

David Siteman Garland.

Formality on social media simply doesn't play. That doesn't mean you need to butcher language, but you can take off your tuxedo. We're all friends here.

Obsess over Small Picture ROI

Some people are obsessed with tracking ROI (return on investment) on everything. Meaning, if they go to the bathroom, they want to know how much money that cost them or made them. Who cares as long as you are moving the sales needle? If you are looking to measure EVERYTHING on social media, you are going to be in for a disappointment. Sure, many things CAN be measured, but the best schmoozers think in terms of the big picture: Is what I'm doing helping my business or hurting it?

A Fluff-Free Story

Personally, social media has been a huge business builder and marketing weapon for me, and I bet it can be for you, too. My first experiences were completely NOT business related and included AOL chat rooms back in the day and MySpace and Facebook in 2004 (when I was an undergrad at Washington University in St. Louis, which happened to be one of the first few schools to get Facebook). In 2006, I was promoting my first company, Professional Inline Hockey Association. Small problem: After spending money on all the things to run a hockey league (jerseys, referees, rinks, entertainment, tickets, and many more goodies), there was no more money. Meaning, I couldn't do any of the things a Goliath company could do. There was no bling for traditional ads or to hire a big PR or marketing firm. Out of necessity, I had to do it myself. I had to market and promote the league in some way and fill the stands.

So, I turned to social media and did my best to do the things listed in this chapter. I connected with hockey fans, influencers, and sponsors—even in the early days of social media, our demographic was big into Facebook and MySpace.

Social media became a channel to connect, promote, market, and chat. Players could interact with fans. Fans could offer suggestions about how to improve the league. Media was shared (photos, videos, and so on) and before long, we had a passionate tribe of inline hockey enthusiasts. Season ticket sales continued to build and attendance rose. We had small, niche buildings to fill and did it via the

Web. This created a David vs. Goliath situation. While other hockey leagues in town (ranging from the NHL to minor league) used the Goliath-like tactics based on money and mass, I used David tactics (funny pun there again, though unintended). The social Web allowed for the players, fans, and league itself to all connect on a scalable one-on-one level.

The same held true when I started *The Rise To The Top*. Here comes some irony. When I started *The Rise To The Top*, I decided to go the traditional route and hustle for a TV show. It was a DIYDSS: Do It Your Damn Self Situation. Meaning, while the show DID air on a local cable network and then a prime spot on ABC, I was responsible for everything and not the network. Everything included production costs, promotion, and everything in between. This ate up my budget completely (budget included my savings plus leveraging some sponsors who has been with me for years to get them involved with the new show).

Back to square one: What is one way to promote a non-boring business show for forward thinkers? Connect with people? Build long-lasting relationships? Oh ... and not spend money. Drum roll please ... social media. Twitter and Facebook quickly became my weapons of choice to connect with guests, sponsors, community members, future fans, and more.

Is social media a magic bullet? Absolutely not. But together with many of the other strategies and ideas in the book you have a smarter, faster, cheaper machine to market, promote, and build relationships.

12

Your Reputation in the Transparent World We Live in

Doing Business Now Is Like Being on Camera 24/7

Smile, you're on camera!

Back, even 10 years ago, people could get away with being douche bags (I know, nice choice of language). Why? Because there were only a few ways they could be "outed" for being jerks.

Perhaps the local newscast picked up something stupid that person did. Or the individual was arrested. Or someone complained to a friend about them over coffee. The outlets for transparency were limited. Only certain people had a voice.

With the Social Web, Everyone Has a Voice

Some voices are large and in charge. Some are a little quieter. But everyone has a say. Instantaneously. Think about this shift for a second. Let's pretend a few years ago you had a bad experience at a restaurant. What could you do? You could tell your friend Jane next time you saw her. E-mail a few friends. Write a letter to the editor of the local food publication. You could do it pretty quickly in private (e-mail, in person) or super slowly in public (letter to the editor).

Now you could tweet it, Yelp it, Facebook it, blog it, make a video about it, whatever. And you can do it as privately or as publicly as you want . . . in a blink of an eye.

The reality is that this shift is going to continue. More people are blogging. More people are on social media sites. More people have a voice. More people are creating and posting instantaneous video with pocket cameras and phones. The world has never been, and continues to get, more transparent and connected. In my opinion, this is a good thing. Nay, an amazing thing. Why?

Because there is nowhere to hide and that is incredible. Good, genuine, kind, caring people are going to thrive (as well as businesses that genuinely care). Those that fake it will be busted one way or another. They might not be exposed today or tomorrow . . . but it will happen at some point. You are leaving your digital footprint every time you hop around the Web. And other people will leave your footprint for you, as well, based on their experiences with you online and off.

Being a good person and doing good business has never been more important, and it is making the world a better place.

Imagine that you are on camera 24/7. Unedited and raw. Would you be happy with what people see?

Watch Your Step

Your Digital Footprint Is Your Reputation

Everything you do online leaves some kind of footprint. It might be long lasting or it might be short lived. Every photo, every message, everything. Now, this doesn't mean you should be paranoid about privacy, but do be aware that the Internet is like a living, breathing encyclopedia of you.

Every little interaction you have—be it small talk, commenting on someone else's website, or your own content—is an opportunity to build your reputation. Are you coming off as a self-centered jerk? A helpful person? A product pusher? A trusted resource? A connector? A sketchy person who goes to a lot of weird parties and posts photos of himself?

When your name comes across someone's screen or phone is the reaction, "Not her again." Or "Sweet, I wonder what she has to say?"

If you want the second reaction to happen more frequently, it is all about reputation. And if you think about it, reputation is marketing. Those with great reputations get the business, are referred, build the brand, and are well liked. That is a great position to be in.

How are you perceived? Online and offline? There has never been more information readily available about, well, everyone, including yourself (have you Googled yourself regularly?).

But the good news is that you can be smarter, faster, cheaper when it comes to creating, monitoring, and improving your reputation and making sure you are known for what you should be known for.

The Keys to a Solid Online Reputation

The Foundation Is Your Brand and Hub

The word "branding" sometimes has a negative Goliath-like connotation. A brand is normally perceived as something a big company does that costs zillions. Or some people view it as a logo.

I would argue that branding is extremely important for entrepreneurs and forward thinkers of all shapes and sizes, and it goes hand in hand with reputation.

Your brand is what you stand for and want to be known for.

Your reputation is how others perceive you and how they talk about you.

Combine the two and you have branding platinum. Think for a second about what happens when these things don't line up. Let's say you visit a guy name Dudley's website on landscaping. The website is really boring, plain, and has little information. It's stuck in a time warp advocating pink plastic flamingos in your front yard. You Google him and can't seem to find anything relevant. Then, a friend tells you that Dudley is the most innovative landscaper around. He knows all about the most amazing plants and watering systems. He is super creative and cutting edge.

Hmmm, something doesn't add up. Dudley has a reputation for being an innovator but his website and Google search don't line up with that recommendation. His brand and reputation don't add up. Same applies offline as well. This isn't just about online reputation.

First and foremost, as previously mentioned, does your online hub (website) convey what you want to the world? Is it you? Does it reflect your personality and brand or is it a blah-fest? Or is it just a template that looks super cheap and feels like everyone else's website?

Think about big brand websites for a second. Many are faceless and slick. Big words. The David advantage over Goliath here is humanizing the business. Show your true colors and build a brand.

Take, for example, Ali Brown. If you are lucky enough to meet Ali, I guarantee you will walk away muttering the same word I did: IMPRESSIVE. Ali is the creator of a multimillion-dollar empire including *Ali Magazine*, Ali Boutique, and other ventures catering to female entrepreneurs. And it all started with just a simple e-zine. Her ever-expanding empire includes events, media, speaking engagements, and many other successful ventures.

Ali also has a great reputation. Search her name and see what appears. Ask people who know her, and they will tell you something positive. And, of course, as she told me, Ali likes to be liked (that is a good thing, although there are a few people out there who love to be hated—I digress).

Ali's brand and reputation are one in the same—holding hands for a stroll in the business park. Ali is fun, personable, glamorous, and helpful. Ali's website, products, and events are all fun, personable, glamorous, and helpful. And, you guessed it, if you search around or ask someone, more times than not you are going to hear that Ali is fun, personable, glamorous, and helpful. Not only is it consistent, but it is authentic. That is who she is and who she wants to be.

Because this brand and reputation is important to Ali, she even has a term for when it strays a little: off brand. For example, if a staff member is wearing . . . um . . . some *less than* glamorous clothing, the individual is reminded that she is a little off brand. Is this being superficial? Not at all. Let's be honest here: Looks are often a big part of a person's first impression about someone else. Is it the only thing that matters? Not at all. But, it is the handshake, the first impression, and the foundation.

Adding Your Voice and Participating

Goliaths have a lot of things to worry about. Sometimes size leads them to worry about the wrong things like how many lawyers to hire for the next lawsuit.

Are you monitoring your niche online and not just your name and your company's name? More importantly, if something pops up that is relevant, do you move in like Rambo and offer a thoughtful comment? (I guess that isn't exactly like Rambo, because your goal isn't to kill people.)

Let's pretend you are in the wedding flower business. You could have a Google Alert (or whatever alert you want) set up for every time someone mentions "wedding flowers" or "wedding flower information" or "wedding flower questions" on the Web. It can be delivered to you however you want: via e-mail or an RSS reader.

When something relevant and interesting comes across your screen, it provides a tremendous opportunity for you to add your thoughts. You can leave an insightful comment on other people's blogs, shows, or online forums.

By becoming part of the conversation on other sites in your niche or related to your niche, you are improving your reputation. Of course, it matters what you say. If you come in and spam and scream about how amazing you are or are off topic, you will hurt your reputation.

There are some great benefits to joining the conversation. For one thing, as we all know, search engines pick up content more than anything else. Therefore, someone might search for "wedding flower help" and end up reading an article on someone else's site entitled "Josie's Guide to Wedding Flower Help." They read the article and then at the bottom there are a few comments. One of them is from you. You offer another piece of advice that adds to the conversation. When you add to the conversation, you get a place to enter your name and website address, which leads back to your hub. Next thing you know a searcher might come find out what else you have to say. You aren't stealing traffic from anyone; you are just participating. This is an added bonus.

Plus, this could help you strike up a relationship with the blogger, which is huge (and discussed in the next chapter).

Among the many people who do this well is Dan Schawbel from Personal Branding Blog, who you met in Chapter 5. Anytime something is mentioned that contains the words "personal branding," Dan is all over it like a kid in a candy store. It might be an article, blog post, show, book, whatever. If it happens, Dan is in there adding to the conversation. And because he is the expert, his comments will certainly be more insightful than what you'd get by "having the intern do it."

Guest Posts/Videos/Articles

Finding sites in your niche that allow guest posting is an incredible way to build community, market and promote, and improve your reputation.

Being a good writer or creator in any medium can qualify you to contribute guest posts. The key here is to be specific and take your same persona to other people's sites—and that means acting as a trusted resource and not a product pusher. Take, for example, Sarah Evans often known even better by her digital name PRsarahevans. Sarah has built up an incredible brand in the PR industry. She does consulting, helps folks with online PR, and is a real influencer when it comes to public relations and journalism. Sarah also has a passionate following that hangs on her every word. Why is this? Why has Sarah become the go-to online PR expert among many other things? Is she some kind of superhuman with magical powers? Or some kind of outlier who happened to be in the right place at the right time? Not to discount Sarah, because she is VERY talented, personable, and a great person, but you really can replicate her success.

Sarah essentially succeeded by being smarter, faster, and cheaper. She decided to become a trusted resource by demonstrating her knowledge to the world and combining those three vital components: passion, personality, and knowledge . . . which led to expertise. Sarah's weapon of choice to achieve this was writing. Sarah researched blogs and different online media sources. She got to know them. She networked online and offline with the people who ran them. Sarah researched each audience and then came up with a unique angle. And then she wrote a guest article. Like everything else online, she started small and reached out to blogs with just a few passionate readers, and then she used each article as a building block for the next and then the next. It led to big opportunities such as writing for the top social media blog, Mashable. Over time her brand and influence began to grow. Every time Sarah wrote an article, a few more people knew about her and perhaps started following her on Twitter or visiting her website (the beauty of instant online links). Her reputation grew one step at a time and one person at a time.

Sarah was able to associate herself with others with a positive reputation and that, in turn, helped her. Something to keep in mind is that Sarah's posts were text-based because that is her comfort medium. You might be better at video or audio, which opens some unique doors as well. Ever thought about doing a guest video post? You might just stick out from the pack.

Negabots and Haterade and Screwing Up

Some people wake up in the morning and drink a bitter glass of Haterade. So remember no matter how pure your intentions or how amazing you are, negabots will rear their ugly heads. They might be against you because you are so damn handsome or pretty. Or because you know a lot and they don't. Or because you are building a great business and they are stuck in a boring job. The list goes on.

The opposite of negabots are people who legitimately have concerns or are upset because you screwed something up. It happens to ALL of us.

Besides having alerts set up for key terms involving your niche, smarter, faster, cheaper entrepreneurs also monitor their own names, business names, and maybe even a competitor or two. This will allow you to keep tabs on conversations.

What is the smarter, faster, cheaper approach to a little damage control? The line between a healthy debate and being a jerk is occasionally a fine one.

The first thing to do is assess the situation: Does this person have a legitimate complaint or is he looking for a fight? It might be hurtful. It might be true. It might be false. My experience has been that it's best not to ignore it. Jump into the conversation in a friendly way. If the person is looking for a fight and you don't rise to the bait, he or she will move on. You essentially kill them with kindness. And if it was a legitimate concern, you have addressed it. Gary Vaynerchuk is the master of this approach. He thanks the criticizer for the comment and responds. Then he moves on.

One time, one of Gary's websites was hacked by an "adult" website. People going to buy some wine were unfortunately greeted with something else. Let your imagination run wild. What did Gary do? Did he hide behind a PR spin agency or a spokesperson? Nope. He got out his video camera, apologized to folks, and that was it. Done and done. Simple, yes. Which begs the question, why don't more people do it?

The high ground is sometimes hard to take, but the view from the top is a lot nicer than getting dragged into a war. You get a voice. You get to participate. Your online actions speak loudly. One year from now when someone discovers a comment you made online, will it be something you wanted to say or was it posted in the heat of the moment?

13 | Respect the Blogger and New Media

We can only say so much about our content, our business, and ourselves without sounding like jerks. Promotion sounds much better when it's coming from someone else, doesn't it? Especially if that person is trusted, respected, and influential.

Remember Bill Gates' famous quote: "If I were down to my last dollar, I would spend it on PR."

That may be great for one of the richest men in the world, but what about the rest of us? Having others talk about you is a huge key to success. It was once as simple as writing a compelling story and then blasting it out with a series of press releases. Now the rules have changed and we can generate interest, exposure, and increase our credibility with a smarter, faster, cheaper approach to PR.

And you can do this all yourself.

So how do you become newsworthy? A quoted trusted resource? A media magnet? How do you leverage each appearance (online or off) to ensure that you win another one? Form REAL relationships with journalists, bloggers, and producers—MUTUALLY BENEFICIAL relationships that benefit both you and the media source (as opposed to a blood-sucking manipulative one)?

Is it more important to focus your time and energy on new media magnets such as bloggers and podcasters, or on traditional media like newspapers, magazines, and TV shows?

The Dumber, Slower, Expensive Goliath Approach to PR

There are a lot of things that hustling entrepreneurs have to get done on a daily basis, so a logical play is to hire a big, fancy PR firm—*if* you can swing the big bucks that it takes.

I'm not saying that there's anything wrong with PR firms. There are some fantastic and innovative ones out there.

Their best, of course, is expensive to buy—thousands of dollars, possibly hundreds of thousands. Sounds like something Goliath might do but not David.

In many cases, traditional PR firms have associations with traditional media sources. Fair enough. But, what about bloggers with passionate audiences? Bloggers who want to hear from YOU and not your mouthpiece? Online media and offline are two different animals—like a zebra and a horse.

The results of hiring a traditional PR firm for your modern company? Maybe an article or an appearance here or there. And maybe not.

It might work. It might not. But it *will* cost you. And if it does work, you have to spend even more money to keep it working.

So, What Is the Smarter, Faster, Cheaper Approach?

As with marketing and building your business, there are do-it-yourself approaches. You are in control. You form the relationships, generate the interest, and pitch reporters who are actively looking for new stories. You show YOUR personality, prove your expertise, and leverage more opportunities for you and your company. You connect one-on-one with bloggers who share your passion and personality.

The smarter, faster, cheaper approach is to put traditional media out of your mind *for now*. Pretend it doesn't exist. Focus on online media sources and bloggers. Podcasters. Online magazines. Shows. Whatever. This doesn't mean traditional media isn't important; rather, it is a shift in mindset.

I hope that didn't make your heart stop beating (if so, please dial 911; thank you). Let me explain.

Finding the Niche Eyeballs

For one thing, and you know this, eyeballs are everywhere these days. Independent blogs and media sources are snatching them up faster than a failed dieter grabs food at an all-you-can-eat buffet. Bloggers have passionate, niche audiences and play by a different set of rules than traditional media.

Bloggers and online content creators are a different breed of folks. If you plan on sending them a bunch of press releases about how awesome your product is, please stop reading, take this book, hit yourself on the head (lightly)—and then continue reading.

There are content creators of all sizes and shapes in almost every niche. Unlike mainstream media, bloggers can laser focus on a niche (just like you can with YOUR online content). Some focus on text; others on video. Some are a mix. But just like you, they are content providers.

They might have a daily or weekly Web show, an online magazine, a news site, or a how-to site.

They might have a website full of interviews, one that has one interesting writer, or many different kinds of contributors.

Positioning yourself as a trusted resource—a person who gives first, an expert, and a content provider—makes it much easier to connect with the influencers in your niche who are doing the same. As long as you are not a product pusher, you have a much better chance to connect with and form incredible relationships with bloggers.

But you know all of this already, right? Especially if you didn't just skip to this chapter and actually read the previous ones (if you did skip—hello and welcome!).

New Media Creators Need to Be Your Best Friend

For one thing, you can find bloggers that have your EXACT same interests and demographic in mind. Your precise niche—not one that sort of fits but an exact match. It doesn't matter what your niche is; someone, somewhere covers it.

The best bloggers and online content creators are excited about their topics, just like you. Nobody told them that they had to blog; they were compelled to do it and fueled by passion, not just money. It isn't like a corporation—an entity that is CLEARLY trying to push its product.

And content creators have an audience and/or a community. It might be big. It might be small. But, I can guarantee it is targeted. It might be left-handed animal lovers. Wine lovers. Or in the case of Dogfiles.com, dog lovers.

The most successful online personalities are also *accessible*. This doesn't mean they are readily available for you to annoy them; it just means that there IS some fairly easy way to get in touch with them. But access is often a double-edge sword, because "easy to contact" means that more people *will*. This, in turn, means that you have to stand out from the oodles of people clamoring for their attention while still respecting their time (more on that soon).

New media and bloggers are genuine, protective, trusted, and influential. They don't promote bad products, services, or people. In truth, no one can save a bad product; this goes without saying. Let's say you are the most likeable person in the history of the world (which you are, right?). You are great on video. You have a fantastic blog with all kinds of great content. Your smile is worth a zillion dollars. You can write with the best of them. You, in short, are utterly awesome.

But your product or service is lacking. It doesn't work. It's confusing, or it doesn't quite do what it claims to do. It lacks originality.

Again, the whole trust factor comes into play here. You are answering to a community, not just an audience—and the media creator has to protect them. If not, *everyone* will look bad. And while it might be possible to sneak past a few people, it won't last. There is no longevity in being mediocre.

Why? Because these communities trust the people they follow. If bloggers and content creators *did* promote shoddy products and lackluster services (which happens accidentally from time to time, of course ... nobody is perfect), then their followers would call them out on it—instantaneously. It's the whole two-way conversation thing. New media allows a person to respond directly—which is a good thing. It keeps everyone honest.

When you form a relationship with a new media person, keep in mind that you are dealing with a person—not some faceless entity. New media folks are social. Interactive. Most are digital citizens who spend a lot of time online, spreading and sharing content. You are forming a one-on-one relationship, not blasting people with press releases. It is about friendship and business. New media tips products more than traditional media.

Two great examples of this are authors Seth Godin and Tim Ferriss.

You have probably heard of both of these best-selling authors. Seth has written 11 books (many of which are best sellers), including some of my favorites: *Tribes, Linchpin,* and *Purple Cow.* Tim wrote the internationally acclaimed *The 4-Hour Workweek.*

Now, keep this in mind while I tell these two stories: The product in both of these cases is a book. Your product probably is not (unless, of course, it is). But insert whatever you like into the story to make it your own. Your product. Your services. Your whatever. It rings true, no matter what you sell.

Tim and Seth both have brilliant marketing minds and are always on the cutting edge. And both men realized that the key to selling more books wasn't just making traditional media appearances and circulating blurbs. Tim's book was and continues to be successful because of relationships he formed with bloggers. He even hired (and then fired) an expensive PR firm to promote his book. He spent thousands of dollars that got him only a couple of articles (the PR firm didn't have a clue about blogger relations). He wasted time and money.

Before *The 4-Hour Workweek* came out, Tim Ferriss was relatively unknown. He attended conferences where bloggers hung out (like BlogWorld), and met bloggers in his niche. He talked about his concept of lifestyle design with folks he knew were interested. Sure, he mentioned the book he had coming out, but he focused on forming genuine relationships. Schmoozing. Networking. Joking around. Becoming likeable. And he maintained these relationships over time and helped promote the bloggers. He *gave first.*

And what do you think happened when his book came out?

Many of these bloggers were now friends with Tim; and, of course, people help their friends. So they blogged about the book; interviewed Tim; posted honest, noncontrived reviews. Some of these bloggers were really big and had thousands of people reading every day. Others were much smaller. But together they comprised a perfect storm to create huge buzz. And that, in turn, created a snowball effect. One of the people who blogged was Robert Scoble, one of the most influential tech bloggers in the world. The mere fact that Scoble had covered the book then led to *more* buzz, which, in turn, elicited traditional media appearances, increased new media appearances, and more. And what were the results? A *New York Times* best seller, an international phenomenon, and the ultimate leverage for Tim.

Tim, himself, is the first to point out that a major lesson from this experience is: Don't come off as a product pusher. Instead, position yourself as a resource with a big idea. Lifestyle design—the notion of creating your dream lifestyle by outsourcing menial tasks—was revolutionary at the time that Tim wrote his book. By promoting the idea as something that would help people, Tim sold *around* his product. He taught, inspired, and entertained; he didn't sell or force a product on others. However, he did *have* the product to support his idea—and it is a good book. If it were terrible, it wouldn't matter how many relationships he formed; it wouldn't have had the same result.

It is safe to say that bloggers are what helped Tim Ferriss become a rock star of a resource.

An equally important, yet slightly different, story is Seth Godin's. Every time Seth releases a new book, he does something unique to let people know about it. For example, when *Purple Cow* came out, he shipped limited-release copies in purple milk cartons.

Linchpin might be Seth's best work yet. He told me during our interview that he put everything into it and has nothing left. Unlike Tim, Seth is already a household name in the marketing world. His blog is one of the top (if not literally *the* top) marketing blogs in the world. Seth could probably land on pretty much any daytime talk show, magazine, or newspaper to promote the ideas in his book. Normally, he would send advance copies to traditional media sources—hoping, of course, that they would review it, write it up, or have him on for an interview.

But for this book—his biggest and most impactful work yet—he did none of this.

He didn't send one single book to a traditional media source—and it still ended up being a *New York Times* best seller (which, while not the only measurement of success by any means, is certainly a significant one).

So, how did Seth go about promoting his work and spreading ideas, as he says, this time?

He went on a Media 2.0 tour from the friendly confines of his office.

Meaning, he leveraged relationships that already existed to be featured on a plethora (haven't used that word in awhile) of blogs, Web shows, podcasts, and other new media sources—ranging from John Jantsch's Duct Tape Marketing to Chris Guillebeau's The Art Of Non-Conformity.

Interviews. Text. Audio. Video (like on my site—I was lucky enough to be part of the tour). Guest blog posts. A whole media mix.

No plane tickets were purchased. No huge PR firm had to pitch him. No time was wasted.

And yes, Seth is a big name. However, he realizes that online content creators are becoming more and more important by the day. More influential. More powerful. More noteworthy.

And the proof is in the buzz and sales. Sounds smarter, faster, cheaper to me.

But what about traditional media?

This isn't to say that traditional media is dead, or that it's a waste of time to reach out to these people. Neither of these points is true. But think about traditional media as the delicious cherry on top of a big bowl of ice cream. Each online media source is a scoop of ice cream. Some online media sources are little scoops (a smaller community with maybe just a few readers). Some are HUGE scoops (maybe even a tub), with a huge community of thousands—or in some cases, millions.

Each time someone mentions you in some capacity online, it is a scoop into your bowl. And these scoops add up over time (as long as you take advantage of them and don't let them all melt). Sometimes you have added so many scoops that you can put a little cherry on top (a traditional media story). And these cherries also have value.

In fact, mainstream media (magazines, TV shows, newspapers, and magazines) are great for:

- Posting a fancy logo on your website or media page, for instance, "As seen on ABC," which is on my site.
- Reaching a different, more mass audience.
- Increasing your value as an expert.
- Providing great conversation topics—and who couldn't use a little conversation? (It sure beats the heck out of talking about the weather, right?)
- Providing print articles that are great for framing and displaying in your office. I have some up on the wall, and I feel like a super cool big shot (hey there, good lookin'!).
- Leveraging even more buzz-building opportunities—as even a little buzz leads to bigger buzz, and bigger buzz leads to MUCH bigger buzz. It keeps growing, growing, growing. So the next time you are talking to a journalist or blogger from a publication or source of *any* size, it is always helpful to mention that you have appeared on/in (insert super important traditional media source here).
- Giving your current clients and/or customers a reason to give you a high-five, as it is another means by which to install confidence in their purchase. "Hey there, Jim. We were just featured on CTRV TV. Check it out!"

Plus, there is another big hidden value here: The online version of the traditional media source.

We are in the midst of the "on demand" generation. Content—when, where, and how you like it—according to *your* demands and *your* schedule.

One good thing is that practically every traditional media source has *some* kind of online edition. It might be the same as the print or TV, or it might be slightly different. But it's always some form of digestible content for you to sample and spread. While people will probably miss your 5 o'clock appearance on the local news, they can watch it online at their leisure when they hear about it from you.

Traditional media CAN help take you to the next level. It should just come later on, as a special bonus.

For example, the previously mentioned Millionaire Matchmaker Patti Stanger credits her ability to get on the map to a magazine article written about her in *Marie Claire* magazine. But it took years and years of dedicated, hard work for her to get to that point—which eventually led to her TV show on Bravo TV. It took several years for her to be discovered, and even more for her to become a TV star. Today, YOU can take control of being discovered.

And even if you don't eat the cherry, the ice cream is still delicious.

Do You Have to Be Sexy to Be Covered?

One of the biggest misconceptions about being covered by all types media is that you have to be "sexy"—meaning that your product has to be something incredibly revolutionary. Or you have to be in an industry where people only attend the coolest parties and drive the most luxurious cars. Or whatever your version of sexy is.

I disagree. Because sexy is in the eye of the beholder (and maybe a little bit in the lighting, too).

Take, for example, Brian Scudamore, founder of 1-800-GOT-JUNK—a company he started in college that now is making over a million dollars every couple days with franchises nearly everywhere. You've probably heard of 1-800-GOT-JUNK and seen one of its big trucks go by, but when I had a chance to interview Brian, I got some interesting—and unexpected—lessons related to passion for one's work and creating buzz.

1-800-GOT-JUNK is a media magnet. It has appeared in online and traditional media over 5,000 times, having been covered by nearly every major and minor news outlet (including my show—I think I made it 5,001). And it is a company that hauls freakin' junk!

What has given it such star power? The answer lies in passion and being aggressive. The company hit the phones and e-mail. Its people called and pitched with energy and enthusiasm. They were excited about their company, and they asked journalists what they were looking for. They formed genuine relationships. They cared about what the journalists wanted. If the journalist wrote about business, they would pitch business lessons from hauling junk. Or if they were talking to someone who covered franchises, they talked about the keys to successful franchising. And guess what? It worked. I'll bet if they didn't have that same level of energy and passion, the number of articles written about 1-800-GOT-JUNK would have been reduced to maybe a couple of hundred, tops.

Besides passion, what are some other ways to stick out even if your industry isn't the most sexy?

Well, for one thing, creating interesting content will separate your company from most others. Perhaps you have a dog food company that does a Web show filming the funniest dog tricks of all time. Or you're a business consultant who does a podcast interviewing two people a week who have miserably failed at business. Or you're the real estate agent who decided not to do it like everyone else and instead launched a daily, MTV Cribs-style blog that features unique homes and quirky commentary like real estate entrepreneur Sarah Bandy.

Of course, the key to this—as we've already discussed—is your online home: your website. Does it differentiate you from your industry? Do you link to every interview or mention of you REGARDLESS of how big or small it is?

Every Blogger and Online Media Source in Your Niche Matters

Could you use one more customer? One more client?

If you just nodded or raised your hand (which would be a bit odd), then think about this for a moment: If you sell soap, every soap blogger is important. If you are a marketing consultant, every marketing blog is important. If you wrote an e-book on elephants, every elephant blogger is important.

And trust me, there is a blog for pretty much everything (if not—then go ahead and create one).

Size Is Overrated, Pay Attention to Small

Liz Strauss—expert blogger and founder of the SOBcon (big business blogger convention)—said it best: "Little bloggers grow up."

Up-and-comers are fueled by passion. They care what people think about them. They are looking to build an audience. They are probably not jerks. They are more accessible (or at least should be). They remember who helped them. They are hustling.

And a lot of little bloggers add up.

It might take more work, but it might work out better. If you want to reach 10,000 people in your niche, there are all kinds of ways to get there.

1 blogger with a community of 10,000 people.

100 bloggers each with a community of 100.

10,000 bloggers each with a community of 1.

You get the idea.

I can share this from personal experience. When I was just starting to build a strong community (about one year into it . . . remember, it takes time), I was connected to *über*blogger Chris Brogan by Lewis Howes (Lewis appears again!). It was one of those funny, quick conversations where I was walking down the street and Lewis called and said at a speed of a million miles an hour, "I've got Chris Brogan on the phone. Here he is."

Realize that this was *huge* for me. Chris is one of the top influential bloggers in social media and what he calls "human business" (great term). He's also one of the founders of New Marketing Labs—a very cool company—in addition to also being a heck of a nice guy who had that new book coming out (*Trust Agents*—which became a *New York Times* best seller). As you can imagine, Chris has a pretty darn full plate. He's constantly blogging, attending and speaking at conferences, consulting, running his marketing company, and, at that point, promoting his upcoming book. That is *a lot* of stuff.

But when I approached Chris and asked if he wanted to come be on an episode of *The Rise To The Top* TV, he enthusiastically agreed. He came into town, and we had a tremendous dinner, interview, and afternoon tea. (Afternoon tea? Really? How proper of us!).

I'll never forget the experience; it was extremely humbling. Why? Because not only did Chris take a good amount of time out of his extremely busy schedule, he also refused to let me pay for his hotel room and airfare, despite my incessant offers. He claimed that he came because he wanted to—not merely because I asked—and the meeting was mutually beneficial. I, an upcoming TV and Web host/writer/interviewer, got one of the most influential social media personalities on my show; and Chris got the chance to meet a community (my audience) he might not have reached before meeting me. And even though we didn't have hundreds of thousands of people watching yet like we do now, Chris identified me as someone with whom he wanted to build a relationship—as I did with him.

We continue to stay in contact online and offline, and help each other whenever we can. Plus, he also knew—via his shiny Chris Brogan crystal ball—that our website was going to gain in popularity. And, as mentioned, online content can increase in value over time. It isn't as if he was JUST going on TV. The video interviews with Chris archived on the site have gotten hundreds of thousands of views well beyond the original airing.

The lesson here is simple: It's potentially futile to always go after *just* the big fish. But forming real relationships never goes out of style.

Where Do You Find New Media Sources?

There are roughly a million ways (no exaggeration here!) to search, find, and identify new media sources. Check out sites like Alltop.com, Technorati.com, and Google Blogsearch to find folks in your niche. New and interesting blogs pop up or are newly discovered all the time. By keeping a finger on the pulse of your industry, you create a substantial knowledge advantage.

I've also noticed that simply paying attention—to social media sites, to what people's favorites are, to the top blogs in your niche and seeing who THEY link to—usually leads to identifying more sources. It is sort of like the red car phenomenon. When you buy a red car, you start noticing all the other red cars on the road, because you are tuned in.

So, tune in to new media. There are some amazingly useful, free resources to check out. One is MediaOntwitter (www.mediaontwitter.com), which is exactly what it sounds like it is. It includes the traditional and new, and it's a great resource to use for making connections.

Another one, previously mentioned, is Peter Shankman's HelpAReporter.com for reporters looking for experts. It is free to sign up, and you receive multiple e-mails a day containing media sources looking for someone who has particular knowledge or experience in a given field, industry, or topic. What was once a hidden, expensive secret sauce is now completely free.

Avoid Rookie Mistakes When Reaching Out to New Media

Mistakes are a good thing. I know, I make them all the time . . . maybe too often. And while learning from them is critical, the following are some ways to avoid making them when striking up relationships with new media folks. I have the weird (though advantageous) position of being on both sides of the table. Meaning, I have people pitching me on stories, while I'm simultaneously attempting to form relationships with other new media (and sometimes traditional) sources. So, I'm speaking here from experience—what I've seen and tasted myself.

Not Knowing the Material

Don't approach people without doing your homework, meaning you haven't read, watched, or listened to the work of the people with whom you're trying to interact. This is definitely dumber, slower, expensive. It's expensive because you risk being exposed by the new media source who might spread the word about your lack of knowledge. (Uh oh!) While that won't hurt your wallet, it *will* hurt something even more valuable: your reputation.

Assuming Everyone Is the Same

There are all kinds of bloggers and online media sources, all with varying personalities, interests, styles, approaches, and so forth. If you assume everyone is the same, you end up in the old "pitch and pray" trap: sending one press release to multiple people and praying that it works, somehow, with at least one of them. Don't do this; instead, customize your approach based on the person you're contacting. You'll have a far better chance of actually piquing someone's interest this way. Make it personal. One-on-one. Show you care.

Using the Wrong Contact Method

While this isn't necessarily a deal breaker, it is important to keep in mind. New media sources are very open about how to get in contact with them. In fact, there is a page with contact information on just about every site. READ THE PAGE. Think about how *you* prefer to be contacted. Do you want to be contacted by phone, or does the sound make you cringe? Is the back-and-forth of regular e-mail too slow for you? Do you prefer to chat live via social media sites? The point is that you likely have a first choice, and so do new media sources. Robert Scoble, for example, responds to public contact (meaning tweets and comments on his blog) before private (such as e-mail). Some people prefer e-mail. Some prefer Twitter or Facebook. You will increase your chance of contacting people if you find out exactly how they *want* to be contacted. And remember not to forget the ultimate way to contact (but not pitch): face-to-face. Are you getting out there and hanging out with new media sources?

Not Respecting Time

Realize that when you send an e-mail, tweet, Facebook message, package in the mail—whatever—to a new media source, these people are busy. They might not respond quickly (or at all). This doesn't mean that you keep doing it. Persistence—perhaps in the form of a follow-up or two—is a good thing. Being pushy and annoying (sending and sending, pitching, begging) on the other hand, is never in style.

And no new (or traditional) media source is going to sift through a *War and Peace*-length e-mail or one that's extremely vague. So be concise, and be specific. Express what you need to say in as few words as possible.

Sending Press Releases

I'd avoid these like a plague, UNLESS a website mentions specifically that it accepts news submissions. If that's the case, try to make it personal. A good example here is Ryan Holmes, CEO of Hootsuite—a unique service that helps people manage their social media sites from a single screen of awesome. Hootsuite has gotten all kinds of great mentions on top social media blog Mashable.com. It's truly a match made in heaven. How did Ryan do it? The story is simpler than you might think. Since Mashable accepts news submissions, Ryan submitted one. But, he divided the submission into two parts. The first part was from Ryan himself and was very personal. The second part was the "additional information" that would make the basis of a good article. I'd argue that this personal touch—along with a quality product, of course—is what allowed Ryan to stand out. The blogger doesn't feel like a message is getting shoved in his or her face. Instead, it sounds more like a personal letter with a note that says, "And if you think that's interesting—well, here's some more."

Offering to Guest Blog for Sites that Don't Do This

Guest blogging. Guest videos. Guest appearances. All are supereffective for building your brand AND helping the new media source. But not everyone does this—and figuring out what the protocol for each individual site is means going back to doing your research. Sure, there is a first time for every-thing; but if the site has 294,985,858,586 posts and NOT ONE of them is a guest post, do you think any of us are spe-cial enough to become the one and only? Sort of like offering meat to a vegetarian. Probably not the best idea. *Know the media source.* I can't emphasize that enough.

Wham, Bam, Thank You Ma'am

If you approach a new media source for a connection because you need something *right away*, this could lead to trouble. Sure, some things are timely; but you have to prove to the source that you aren't just in it for your own gain. How can you be of help? That should be the first question you try to answer.

Grow a Bigger Mouth

New media sources *love* people with big mouths—people who tell their friends and who promote the heck out them. They especially love people who do it not only when they are featured, but all the time.

Keep this in mind as you grow your network. The more people that are engaged with you, the better. There's really no sugarcoating it; an engaged network is lucrative for a new media source that is going to cover you.

Also remember: Bigger doesn't necessarily mean engaged. It is really easy to get a bigger network. Just buy some terrible spam program that gets you a bunch of Twitter followers. Or just add random people on Facebook all day to create the illusion of importance.

But, we are all smart. We can tell who is faking it and looking for a quick buck and who is really a genuine person.

Delicious Cherries

If you are helpful and genuine, form relationships, and add a ton of value to the new media source's life, then good things will happen. Of course, it will take some time, but when you have a suggestion—for example, a new product coming out or an idea that can help both of you—these people will listen to you. Not as a stranger, but as a trusted friend.

And all of this ice cream can lead to cherries. What is more compelling to traditional media? Someone who claims to be an expert or someone who can demonstrate his expertise both by what he has created (content) and what others (bloggers, new media sources, and so on) have said about him.

Making yourself an available expert for other new (and traditional) media sources is absolutely crucial to bringing new people to your site. The more good content you create and share, the more leverage you will have when reaching out to others.

Traditional media loves experts, pundits, and effective communicators.

For example, I love functional technology and business—stuff that is easy to use and doesn't take a genius to figure out. So, I suggested to *Great Day St. Louis*, a popular local cable program, that I could be their business and technology expert. I was able to provide videos of my show, articles I'd written on other sites that I contributed to, like Small Business Trends, and a pressroom full of coverage on blogs and other sites. Now, I appear on the show every six weeks to talk about unique topics. It is really fun, and it serves as a way to market both myself and *The Rise To The Top*.

Now, imagine if I had approached the producers of this program from the nontrusted-resource perspective, and said, "Hi guys, can I come onto *Great Day* and promote my resource for forward thinkers called *The Rise To The Top*? It is really great and amazing. You'll love it, I promise!" Nope. Wouldn't work.

The opportunity is there to connect with media sources like never before. Time to start extending a hand.

14

How to Connect with Anyone You Want

Using Your Content, Connections, and Products as a Handshake

Okay, so there might be some people you can't connect with online in one way or another, directly or indirectly. Dead people, and um . . . that is pretty much it.

Thought-leaders, bloggers, potential business partners, sponsors, big companies, small companies, investors, your potential clients, elves, whatever—everyone, for the most part, is online these days. If the person you want to contact isn't online, someone in his or her circle certainly is (assistant, close friend, or if they outsource things . . . a PR or marketing company). If the person has ANY connection to the Internet, there is an opportunity to connect with him. I don't care how busy he is or how many gatekeepers are trying to keep you from him.

Imagine that two people—with whom you have no connection whatsoever—are trying to meet you. Yes, *you*. They want to form a relationship with you out of thin air. Let's call person number one Jane. Jane cold calls you and/or e-mails you and tries to set up a meeting or a phone call. But you can tell that Jane is a product pusher. She is trying to sell you something, and you're unclear about exactly what she wants. Plus—as I mentioned before—she has absolutely no connection to you.

Would you take the call? Would you respond? Or would you be put off?

Now, contrast that with person number two, Sheila. Sheila sends you a card and a gift—something valuable. Some shiny new thing you wanted. Albeit small, it is a gift that helps your business in some form or fashion. The card she sends simply introduces herself and tells you to enjoy the associated gift. Her contact information is at the bottom of the card.

What would you do? Would you ignore her as you did with Jane? Or would you maybe pick up the phone or send an e-mail to thank her for doing something nice?

I don't know about you, but I would certainly be intrigued by Sheila. Who is she? Why did she send me something? What is her story? What does she do?

She used a present as a handshake—and you can do the same with your online content.

Now, let's translate the above scenario to the online world. Jane sends you a product pitch or just wants to meet via e-mail or social media sites. Sheila, on the other hand, reaches out and shares with you an article she wrote promoting you and your company. Perhaps it covers the lessons she learned from you, reviews your product, or provides links to your website.

Whatever the exact subject matter is, Sheila provided value to you right away. Why? Because online content is valuable, and her promoting you is a good thing. As a result, more people are likely to visit your site or find out about you. I don't know any successful person who doesn't want to be mentioned by others in a positive light. It can only lead to good things.

When you use your content and relationship-building skills to promote others, you are essentially opening up a relationship with a present. Not a manipulative present, mind you—but something that could lead to a friendship, or at least get you through the door of someone you meet. And, of course, what you offer has to stick out, be unique, and show that you've put some effort into it. Half-baked cookies aren't really a present, are they?

Plus, a bonus here in the online world is that more people are monitoring their online reputations (you didn't skip the last chapter, right?). And if you aren't, you should be. Start today, in fact. There are all kinds of free (and paid) ways to do this. Free tools like Google Alerts, Google Blogsearch, BackType, Twitter Search, IceRocket Blog Search and others allow anyone to keep a running tab on keywords associated with their company. And, of course, there are comprehensive paid tools such as Radian6, which is like your own search engine and consistently searches social media sites, blogs, chat forums, websites, and more for your name or your business' name.

For example, anytime my name—David Siteman Garland—pops up anywhere on the Internet, I receive alerts that let me know about it. I know that if my name comes up, I'm going to want to check out where and why.

This builds on the notion of reaching out to people to give them a present. Because of alerts, the present may just make itself appear—kind of like a surprise party for the person you're promoting.

The bottom line is that by creating content that promotes others, you have a reason to contact them. What you do with the relationship from there is up to you. Of course, it would be a rookie mistake to give a present and then try to sell someone something. That, my friends, is called a Trojan horse. And nobody likes a Trojan horse, do they?

The steps are simple. Your success will be based on how genuine (and creative) you are.

1. **Give first**. If you have a blog, write about the people you are trying to meet. Review their books or products, tell us five things you learned from them, or write about the three reasons you would like to meet with them. Put it out there.

2. **Reach out**. Send the people you are trying to meet a note in the form of an e-mail or via another social media route. One key here is to try to know them as well as you can before you actually *know* them. In other words: Do they even like receiving e-mail? Are they active on various social media sites? Do they have a preferred contact method? It can't hurt to try different ones, but the more you know early on, the further

ahead you will be. Introduce yourself briefly and share the content. If you aren't communicating directly with the person (and are going through a gatekeeper or assistant), ask that person to pass it on to Ms. or Mr. Important-Enough-to-Have-a-Gatekeeper.

3. **Ask for NOTHING**. This VERY critical step is frequently overlooked. The difference between a present and a secret bribe: The more you give away, the more you will receive.

   A secret bribe has a forced agenda. It makes someone feel as though they HAVE to do something. It forms a relationship based on money and not trust. I've gotten lots of bribes in the mail (unfortunately, no money). They just don't work. It gives you that ewww-I'm-being-used feeling.

   If you want to bribe someone, then go ahead and offer a bribe. I'm not saying it is going to work, but lay out your cards. I will give you this: If it works for everyone, you have a winning situation. If it doesn't, however, you are screwed.

   A present, on the other hand, is much better. A present creates an accidental obligation that isn't forced (which is kind of funny, if you think about it). In literal terms, let's say you sent me a present for my birthday (which is April 19th, by the way, in case you want to note that on your calendar). You probably wouldn't send the present with a note saying something like:

   "David,

   Enjoy this supercool present. By the way, my birthday is June 27th. Here is my address.

   Opportunistically yours,

Ima Sleaze"

That is the tit-for-tat bribery obligation. Yuck.

However, if you just give the gift freely, there is a greater chance for reciprocation of some form. And, you've generated goodwill, which is priceless.

"Hi Betty Sue,

I thought you might be interested in this. Enjoy!

Your pal,

Joe S."

Now you've generated some goodwill. I know it sounds counterintuitive, but when you ask for nothing, you get everything. It's kind of funny the way it works.

I guarantee things will come around as a result. Karma goes to work. The person may or may not offer to do something for you. But either way, you have provided interesting content to your community and opened the channels of communication. Sure beats a pinch on the arm!

Enabling Others to Promote Your Work

You can't go at this alone. If all you do is talk about yourself and how fantastic your business is, it will be impossible to gain long-term traction (unless you are some sort of magical wizard or something). The best way to enable others is to give credit. People like a little love—especially if it is genuine and useful.

For example, I once wrote a post called "The 35 Unique Entrepreneurs That Are Changing the Business World." It was a post that was shared MANY times—because it was about others and not just me. The idea here was simple. I created a list of amazing people and wrote about why I liked them. Then, I shared it on social media sites. After it was out there, I contacted all 35 people one way or another to tell them about it. Some I e-mailed. Some I tweeted. Some I contacted on Facebook. A few I actually called on the phone (I know—crazy, right?). I didn't ask them to do anything. I didn't say, "Hi I wrote this post so you will become my friend." Or, "Hi, I wrote this. Promote it or I will hate you." That would be just sketchy. And it would create one of those tit-for-tat relationships, which just doesn't work. The interesting thing, though, is that almost all 35 people promoted it one way or another. This caused a viral explosion. Cool. But it goes even deeper than that; what I essentially did (and anyone can do the same) is used content as a handshake—a relationship builder, a present. Seth Godin calls this a gift in *Linchpin*. For the people I already knew who I put on the list, it was a great way to stay in contact with them. For the people I didn't know, it was a great introduction (and it's probably not a coincidence that since that post went live, nearly all 35 people have been guests on my show).

The lesson here is simple: When you mention someone or something in a post, *tell them about it*! Don't stalk them with multiple e-mails and Twitter messages; send a quick note to let them know immediately.

The Nametag Guy Scott Ginsberg taught me this one: Send a quick note with the link thanking them for the inspiration.

And guess what? Good things will happen. Karma does exist. Your gesture will end up coming back to you in one way or another. And yes, you might give more than you receive, but what is wrong with that? To me, that seems like a really good thing.

Blogger and New Media Source Relations

Give a Present

Okay, let's face it. We all want *something*. Fair enough, no need to hide it. But to get what you want, you have to give first and put yourself in new media's shoes. As we've already discussed, asking how these sources can help you is the wrong question. You need to ask, instead, how you can help them. What exactly do they want?

Now, everyone is different. Not every new media source wants the same thing. But most of them do have a few things in common.

I've yet to hear of any new media source who wants a smaller audience. Therefore, it's always beneficial to introduce your network to the source. You can send a tweet, an e-mail, or post something on your blog. Find some way to promote the source. It doesn't matter if your network is 2 people or 2,000,000; you are still adding value, and the only cost is your time and a little effort.

This is helpful in two ways. One, you are educating and helping YOUR network around your subject of interest—which can only lead to good things. Let's say that you sell gourmet potato chips. You discover a chip blogger's website, and you spread the word about it. You blog yourself and e-mail folks about this really great find. You give the blogger some recognition. This—sharing what you've learned about the world of chips—is a lot more effective in terms of building your community than bragging about how addictive your gourmet chips are.

Second, you just did something nice—and niceness over time is rewarded. It *will* get noticed, because new media people pay attention. We know when our names pop up online. We know when someone says something positive. You aren't sitting at home in front of the TV and saying, "Boy, I love this show!" You are telling your network about it with one click of the mouse: word of mouth.

Cash Money and Creative Ideas

While guest blogging is great for sites that allow it, there are also some other ways to build a mutually beneficial relationship with bloggers and new media sources. Of course, money is important; we're all in business, right? There are some opportunities to advertise and sponsor new media sources (in fact that gets its own chapter! Who would have thought?). The best part about new media advertising and sponsorships is that they can be extremely creative, and they *really* work. They reach the exact niche you want and aren't limited to normal junk like blinking banner ads. (By the way, if you contact a blogger who ONLY wants to sell you banner ads—RUN. Grab your computer and get as far away as possible!)

And you might be able to get supercreative and create a triangle of new media awesomeness (trust me here). Perhaps you offer the blogger/new media source a special deal for their community for your product or service, and they get a percentage of sales. So, the new media source plugs you in some form or fashion and receives a commission on any sales. And their community gets a deal. And you get the sale. Everyone wins and hugs each other.

Yes, new media sources love free goodies—*if* they are relevant. Don't send mustard to the ketchup blogger. And the bigger the source, the more goodies they receive—so your gift has to stick out. And remember, if you give something to a media source, that doesn't mean the source is obliged to write about you or fly across the country and give you a slap on the back—although the person very well might. And, if a blogger does review your gift, talk about it, whatever—she must disclose the fact that you gave it to her—which is a good thing. It's sort of like ethical bribing (an oxymoron, I know). If anything, it is a free gift. And that's always good. Of course, this doesn't mean that if you send 100 presents, you will receive 100 presents. But you might receive 50. Or 25. Or who knows? But if you give away, you will receive—and I don't just mean products. This applies to anything that might be valuable to someone else—the content you create (if you choose to create, which I hope you do), the introductions you make, the help you provide to others, and the questions you answer. Give it away—and do it often.

15 | Traditional Advertising Is Dying

The Rise of Creative Paid Sponsorships and Social Marketing

The most effective form of advertising is content.
—John Jantsch, *The Referral Engine*

Is the 30-second ad dead? What about print ads? Banner ads? Are they all just on life support? Short answer: pretty much—because consumers have to be interrupted by ads, and almost everyone hates interruptions (I know I do. Don't you?)—especially when a company is essentially guessing that

193

its product just *might* appeal to you. Does it still work for mass-Goliath-marketing? To some extent—but make no mistake, it is fading fast.

Like everything in marketing—and in life—it is time to evolve.

Advertising and sponsorships are not *dead*. In fact, they can still be one of the BEST ways to market and promote your business, along with creating your own content. But the mediums and messaging by which this information is conveyed have changed—for the better.

There's now a tremendous opportunity for entrepreneurs and other people traditionally too small to advertise and sponsor (the Davids of the world) to jump into the game.

With evolution comes new ideas and the rise of creative paid content, which is essentially advertising your *expertise* and having another trusted resource plug your products and services. The best part, of course, is that it's FAR less expensive, much more effective (you don't pay for the 98 percent of people NOT interested in you; you pay for the 2 percent who ARE) and well . . . smarter. And it is long-lasting and social. It lives and breathes. Plus, it is hypertargeted and doesn't work just for random products like soap. It works business-to-business AND business-to-consumer. Sweet.

But first, let's review: What is the point of advertising and sponsorships? It is intended to promote and cause action (word of mouth). Understanding advertising and sponsorships is really simple. The original idea behind it is to promote your product/service/whatever to a target audience.

The purpose of an ad is to convince people that they need your product—with the hope being, of course, that people BUY something at some point.

But nobody likes a product pusher or being sold to, right?

There is a fundamental shift taking place in advertising right now—from product pushing to promoting content and you as the trusted resource. The goal here is for the audience or community to take some kind of action—maybe to read; watch; listen to a piece of valuable, interesting content; which, in turn, might prompt them to visit your website, sign up for your newsletter, friend you on social media sites, stop by your offices, pick up the phone, or download your e-book. Essentially, you are advertising your expertise and letting trusted bloggers and new media sources promote your products and services—a blend of advertising, word of mouth marketing, and public relations.

Now, there are some reasons other than selling that drive people to purchase advertising and sponsorships. Some companies want to be associated with a particular cause or event, so they sponsor it. However, there are problems with traditional advertising that include the following issues.

Risk versus Benefit

It is expensive to experiment in this way. A three-million-dollar Super Bowl commercial; a tiny print ad in a local business paper that costs seven thousand dollars for one week; a one-hundred-thousand-dollar billboard. These all sound like really great ideas ... *IF*:

The three-million-dollar Super Bowl ad generated four million dollars in sales.

The seven-thousand-dollar business paper ad generated ten thousand dollars in sales.

The one-hundred-thousand-dollar billboard generated one hundred and fifty thousand dollars in sales.

But you don't know if it will work *unless* you spend the money. And even then, do you have the measures in place to prove it did or didn't? And I'm not talking about the person who sold you the ad coming back to you and saying how many people saw it. I'm talking about some kind—ANY KIND—of result.

I know that as a scrappy entrepreneur, I can't afford to take those kinds of risks. They are unnecessary—especially when there are better alternatives rising to the surface that cost just a fraction and offer all kinds of additional benefits that traditional ads won't.

Bye-Bye Eyeballs

Traditional advertising is a numbers and eyeballs game. But as we all know, the numbers are moving—because eyeballs are shifting. Everything is becoming more fragmented. Instead of the big players in town controlling all the eyeballs, there are now a series of niche players commanding passionate audiences and attention—competing with the big boys, and earning attention.

It's less mass-based on HUGE numbers, and more niche-based on passion and smaller numbers.

There used to be just a few channels on television, then there were a few more. Then there were hundreds, with more popping up every day. Now there are even *more*—plus thousands of niche online TV shows on pretty much every subject imaginable, from painting your walls to raising prize llamas. The same thing is true with print (which has become online text) and with radio, as well.

And, along with this trend of fragmentation comes passionate niche creators and audiences made up of people REALLY interested in a specific subject or topic—as opposed to companies trying to promote something that is supposed to have mass appeal.

Examples:
- A show focused on business vs. a show focused on passionate entrepreneurs looking to grow their companies.
- A show on technology vs. one focused on tech for moms.

MORE people are online and consuming content they are passionate about. MORE people are on social networking sites sharing with each other. MORE niche shows, blogs, and podcasts are popping up all over the place and attracting eyeballs.

As the shift continues, the dollars will follow. And it isn't about big numbers. It is about laser cutting to reach the EXACT audience you care about.

We are a sharing society. People love to collaborate with each other, and word of mouth, e-mail, and social media have made it fantastically simple to do so. One click and an article—or a link to a video or audio clip—is passed on.

But do you know what isn't shared? Traditional ads.

When is the last time you e-mailed someone to tell them about an awesome ad you saw in some magazine? Or called someone after seeing a really great commercial? Or you cut out a print ad, scanned it, e-mailed it, or put it in an envelope and mailed it to someone? Or took a photo of a billboard or bus stop ad and sent it to someone?

Ridiculous, right?

Sure, there are occasional examples of remarkable ads that *do* spread. Apple, for example, has very clever Mac vs. PC ads that are worth watching. When Anheuser-Busch was in its heyday with creative genius Bob Lachky at the helm (Budweiser Frogs, Real Men of Genius, Wassssup? campaigns), its commercials also spread like wildfire. Bob told me that the Internet provided a new, unofficial medium for them with all kinds of parodies. Sometimes really bad ads also spread, as well. (Search for "Montgomery Flea Market" and you will see what I mean.)

And those stories of remarkable ads are fantastic. But they are rare—REALLY rare. There are hundreds of thousands of ads produced a year. Those that win the ad lottery might cause parodies and buzz—but at a large expense.

Okay, enough ripping the traditional ad world. This book is all about forward-thinking ideas that DO work. There has to be something better than this for folks who want to advertise and sponsor something, right?

What is the replacement?

The Rise of Creative Content Sponsorships and Social Marketing

We all share content—not banners or faceless ads. Most people are more likely to click on products that have been reviewed by trusted sources. Or click on sponsors/advertisers of sites that are displayed in other ways, such as integrated into the content or sponsoring a series.

For example—I like watching hockey, but I don't like beer. Well, somewhere along the way, beer companies got the idea that all hockey fans are males who like beer. Therefore, they run beer commercials during games. Simple enough. But I—and many other people, I'm sure—don't fit into this category. Beer companies made an assumption—one that, in my case, was incorrect.

Nowadays—with tons of niche shows and online resources—marketers have the opportunity to be *much* more creative.

For example: That same beer company discovers five well-known beer blogs and a single online TV show centered on beer. It approaches both the blog and show owners, and comes up with the following creative strategy:

1. The beer company will write three guest blog or monthly posts for each beer blog and will pay the blogger—similar to the way in which it would pay a TV station to run ads. This relationship—which will be disclosed—will create valuable content agreed upon between the beer company and the blogger.

2. The beer company pays the online TV show in one of two ways:

   A. It gives beer to the host and tells him that if he doesn't like it, he doesn't have to market it. But if he *does* like it, he will pay X dollars (or a percentage of sales, affiliate-style) to have a host mention in each episode: "Today's Beer TV is brought to you by Example Beer. I've tried it, I like it, and I won't promote a lousy product on the show. Head to examplebeer.com for 10 percent off a case and try it today."

   B. Another tactic would be for someone from the beer company to appear on the show to offer valuable content to the viewers and market the beer company for a charge. This is a pay-to-play model. For example, the host interviews a beer company representative who offers five tips for avoiding going to the bathroom too much when drinking beer. This both promotes the company and gives viewers valuable content. Everyone wins.

Again, the key in all of this is integrity on all sides. Always disclose sponsorships and remember that the audience comes first.

Here is another example: Let's say you wanted to advertise your monkey training services. The old-school way of thinking would be to try to figure out where the monkey owners MIGHT be—watching *Animal Planet*, for example. So, you would have to purchase a big ad campaign with *Animal Planet*—confined, of course, to 30-second ads—that cost hundreds of thousands of dollars to reach the 1 percent of the audience (or less) that is potentially interested in monkey training. For the sake of argument, let's say that 1 percent is 10,000 people. So you spent roughly $100,000 to reach those 10,000 interested people.

Or, you could go with a much more effective alternative: You find a blogger, online TV show, or Web resource specifically geared toward monkey lovers—people who live and breathe monkeys. They create articles with monkey-owning tips. Video product reviews. Provide interviews with . . . um . . . monkeys.

They have an audience of 5,000, and for $2,500 they provide you—the monkey trainer—with the following:

- An appearance on their weekly Web show to give monkey-training tips.

- The host plugs your product and invites people to go to your site for more information and also to buy monkey-training lessons from you. The plugs are linked into 20 of their articles and their show, which syndicates on social media sites, e-mail, RSS, and more. It is sharable and spreadable.
- All the content with your plugs included is uploaded to a variety of video sites, which you can then put on your site—where it stays up forever.

There are offline advantages to this partnership as well. Even though new media sponsorships are based in the online world, they don't necessarily have to stay there. There may well be ways in which you can extend your involvement—including live events, meet-ups, conferences, and other interesting ways to go from online conversations to real-life interactions.

So—which of these methods would *you* prefer to give the ol' college try?

A Fluff-Free Story

No, this isn't bunny fluff and theory. I've had some experience in this area, and the following are my philosophies on advertising/sponsorships from a content creator perspective.

1. It is of utmost importance to **establish trust with the community/audience**. Trust is hard to gain and easy to lose. If you promote bad stuff, overly

(*continued*)

(Continued)

promote, or promote in a distasteful way, you will lose trust. And once lost, trust is INCREDIBLY hard to get back.

2. Only discuss/display products and services **you feel comfortable promoting**. This advice is inspired by Leo Laporte of *This Week in Tech*, who only promotes things he knows, trusts, uses, or would use. I try to do the same myself, and, as a result, sometimes have to turn down advertising.

3. Make it **more of a partnership** than a passive relationship. A partner is a friend whose interests are linked together with yours. Lazy advertising doesn't fall into the partnership category.

4. **Know that you're running a trusted lab**. Make it experimental. Overdeliver and always be honest. When I work with our sponsors, I try to approach marketing like a lab. Some things will work really well, while some things won't work at all. The idea is to keep trying different things with the end goal of moving the sales needle. The key is to keep everyone's best interests in mind: your audience, advertiser, and of course, yourself, as well.

5. **Provide full disclosure**. If something is sponsored, I say it. If I forget to say it (stupidly), then I'll write it. Just because something is sponsored doesn't alter the impact of the content.

Although I've done it in the past before really diving into these changes, my organization has found great success in abandoning old-school advertising methods.

So, what do we do on *The Rise To The Top*? Something we call "Content Sponsorships" where we work with a variety of budgets. As the name might suggest, our sponsorships are focused around content and knowledge. These experts are usually entrepreneurs who are looking to reach other entrepreneurs (a match made in heaven). Our team sells several packages with elements including:

- An opportunity for the sponsors to tell their stories on *RISE* via an interview with me. This isn't sales pitch BS. Instead, it is an exchange based on education: lessons learned, failures, tips, and of course, a description of how they help people. It isn't scripted or predetermined in any way; it's authentic, done on the spot, and real. Storytelling creates a personal connection, especially since most of our sponsors are entrepreneurs themselves.
- St. Louis-based sponsors have an opportunity to speak on their topic of expertise at a St. Louis *RISE* Lunch. Again—this is NOT a sales pitch. The goal here is to educate the audience and, of course, generate business from those who you discover are the right fit as a result of speaking to them. If people know, like, and trust you, they will do business with you. Nothing beats face-to-face interaction—plus, the event is recorded and shown online as well.

(continued)

(*Continued*)

- Participation in a Tip Series that we develop for professionals based on their skills and knowledge in a given area. This new tactic has worked incredibly well for our long-term sponsors, such as entrepreneur/lawyer Jeff Michelman from Paule, Camazine & Blumenthal P.C. Each sponsor creates with me a series of tips and/or short, unique videos based on their area of expertise that's useful for our audience. For example, they give advice on customer service, marketing, sales, entrepreneurship, productivity, SEO, online marketing, and much more. This is what we call "selling around your product" as previously discussed. Sure, they want to generate business from it (that's the reason why someone would purchase a sponsorship); however, the primary idea here is to *educate,* not to hard sell. If you like a particular business or professional, or want to find out more about them, you can check out their websites, products, services, or e-mail them.
- Plugs. I personally plug sponsors, usually at the beginning and end of our episodes. The purpose is to point people toward their content or product.
- A chance to engage in outside-the-box activities and programs. Because I aim to always do business with people I would refer—and because I like making referrals and helping people, this is an unwritten bonus that I just sort of throw in. I recommend our sponsors (again—ALWAYS disclosing that they

ARE a sponsor—no BS here) to those who might need help in a specific area, since I get e-mails with related queries all the time. Someone looking for an IP lawyer? Of course I will recommend Jeff Michelman; I trust him, I use him myself, and he is a sponsor. This isn't in the contract, but as far as I'm concerned, it's just logical.

These methods have worked for the variety of industries spending money with us: automotive, Internet marketing firms, restaurants, business services, a high-end printer, law firm, tech companies, and many more.

Well, enough about me. The point to take away from these stories is that the advertising and sponsorship game is changing. You can take part in it either by selling sponsorships for your content or, of course, sponsoring or advertising a blog or show that fits with your demographic (or both). And it couldn't be more exciting.

Alternative Forms of Advertising, Sponsorships, and Promotions that Actually Work

I love this description from Peter Shankman's Help A Reporter Out. HARO sends out three e-mails a day (to a very engaged audience), and at the top of each are advertising and sponsorships that Peter sells. These plugs—which Peter writes himself—work well for those looking to reach his very active community. He describes these sponsorships as follows:

"Reach is one thing. Access is another. Audience and one-to-one introductions are a whole different ballgame. HARO sponsors aren't interested in 'how many eyeballs will see this?' or 'how many unique visitors can you expose my brand to?' HARO sponsors want buyers. Engaged, active members of a community who will read their ads, listen to our unique perspective on the sponsor's offer, and then take action and buy something.' HARO's unmatched open rates mean a TON of people are reading your ad and seeing what you have to offer. Period." (Source: www.helpareporter.com/sponsors.)

This all comes back to the importance of metrics. Forgive me if I sound like I'm teaching a course in business school for a moment. There are both hard and soft metrics—both of which are important for measuring effectiveness of paid campaigns.

Soft metrics are non-direct-sales measurements that are relevant and worth purchasing in many cases. A few examples include:

- Facebook fans gained over time.
- Twitter followers gained over time.
- E-mail subscribers increased.
- Number of e-books downloaded.
- Website traffic.
- Video views.
- E-mails received.
- Number of times the content was shared.
- PR opportunities generated.
- New relationships formed.
- People who have been exposed to your brand.
- Your ranking higher on Google for a key phrase and drawing Web traffic from it.

Hard metrics are the things that move the sales needle one way or another. Some come as a result of the soft metrics, and may not happen for a while, whereas some could be immediate. They occur when customers take actions like signing up for a free trial of some kind or purchasing a product/service/whatever. Or they happen when you garner revenue as a result of campaign.

And it's that simple.

Sponsoring online content creates new long-term relationships. You might gain a few new followers—one of whom may, six months from now, buy $10,000 worth of stuff from you. And the entire campaign cost you $2,500. Worth it? I think so. And even more benefits come your way over time.

It isn't like instant oatmeal; creative content sponsorships are long-term relationships and can be measured over the long haul. For example, we just discussed HARO—an organization whose model I love. Each e-mail has a single ad, written by Peter Shankman in his own voice (although you can send him the information you'd like included, he puts his unique spin on it). Peter's community trusts him, and the result is that people read what he writes. They buy stuff he recommends. And it doesn't cost an arm and a leg. At print time, a HARO ad costs under $2,000. It's fairly amazing.

Jason Sadler is a creative genius when it comes to advertising as well. He started I Wear Your Shirt (www.iwearyourshirt.com), a company where customers pay him to wear any shirt they choose, promoting the heck out of a product/service/whatever. You pay him, and he creates and spreads content all day long. Videos. Photos. Blog posts. He has a growing following on social networks.

And his organization has an interesting price structure. It increases every day of the year. The first year he did it, it cost

$1 to hire him on January 1, January 2 was $2, and it went all the way to December 31, which was $365.

Now Jason has a "mini me" also wearing shirts. The price for the service doubled, since customers now had two guys wearing shirts and promoting their business. Knowing Jason, I'm fairly certain that this is only going to increase until he has a small army of people promoting various companies and creating interesting content.

(By the way, I recently gave Jason an idea: I Wear Your Underwear. Well, maybe that isn't such a good idea . . . I guess the audience is slightly more limited. Hmm.)

As I mentioned earlier, with new media sources and bloggers come some incredible opportunities. MyMommy Manual.com co-founder Ria Sharon shared an inside look at some of the opportunities that have worked well—both for My Mommy Manual and for their sponsors.

They have their own expert program called Expert Mommies (doctors, educators, coaches, and so on) who promote to mommies and are also moms themselves. They also partner with companies offering mom products, offer guest posts for mommy-friendly product sites, throw events in online AND offline (including babyshower.20 which took place online and a Mompreneur Pajama Party).

This is obviously a short list of interesting new media sponsorships ranging from expert programs to written articles to e-mail plugs to a guy who will wear your face on his shirt. But, this is where things are heading. A new model based on scalable one-on-one relationships and your expertise and handshakes from content creators. How can you capitalize on it?

16 | Take It Offline

Sure, technology makes things easier. But remember: becoming a smarter, faster, cheaper trusted resource takes place as much offline as it does online.

Much of online networking, brand building, marketing, and promoting actually happens offline. Away from the computers and phones. In the real world (insert scary music here). And, these offline opportunities go hand-in-hand with online opportunities.

The online and offline worlds aren't two different, scary places that are engaged in some kind of sci-fi battle with each other. They work together and enhance each other. Online opportunities create offline opportunities, and vice versa.

The dumber, slower, expensive approach is to draw lines in the sand and take the stereotypical approach by making the following distinctions:

An online business is a tech-heavy organization run by evil and sketchy *über*nerds and ripped-jean kids in Silicon Valley, who don't care about humans, hate customer service, and are looking for the quick buck.

An offline business is old-school and run by people clad in pleated pants (or skirts?) who've never heard of the

Internet(s), are eager to retire, and who hate "those kids and their damn technology."

Despite what many people seem to believe, your company can't be either an online *or* an offline business. You are—you *have* to be—both.

The smarter, faster, cheaper approach: Take your online brain and your offline brain and make them hug . . . like they mean it. Seriously.

Becoming a trusted resource gives you the incredible opportunity to leverage your influence into speaking opportunities and offline events where you gather like-minded people.

Can You Bring People Together?

Bringing people together in real life is an incredibly effective smarter, faster, cheaper strategy. If you think about it, it is the same strategy that you execute online, because you are:

1. Helping people by offering content (an event).
2. Introducing people to one another and helping network and build relationships—both with you and others.

There are several ways to do it.

The dumber, slower, expensive way might be to start by putting on a complicated conference. Sure, it can be done, and many people do it really well; but it takes a lot of work and up-front capital. Dealing with vendors, venues, sponsors, big marketing campaigns to get people there, speakers, the list goes on (trust me . . . I've put on some WAY overcomplicated events in the past and cried myself to sleep for weeks beforehand . . . and sometimes after).

How can you bring people in your niche together? It can be something really simple like a meet-up, or perhaps some kind of unique book club—who knows? It doesn't have to be a huge production. It might just be a lunch or a cocktail hour. Maybe you can bring in a speaker or two or speak yourself.

It is no surprise that super connector Lewis Howes does this extremely well, and live events have been a massive brand builder for him. He started LinkedWorking events where he invited people from LinkedIn to mingle in real life. The idea was simple and it worked. Lewis started doing them in Ohio and then expanded into a few other markets.

Live events are brand-building beasts in the era of the social Web. Think about pre-Internet events. You got an invitation in the mail, you showed up, and maybe you told a friend about how great or awful it was. Maybe a photo or two from the event appeared in your local paper. And that was pretty much it.

Now, people are tweeting about the events they are about to attend. Connecting with other attendees on Facebook. Shooting videos of the speakers with their phones and pocket cameras. Updating people during the event. And this continues after the event as well. Photos and videos are posted online. New connections are made. Relationships are extended.

Plus there is an incredible content opportunity here. If you have speakers or talks at your event, you can have them taped and repurposed online. Those who missed the event can catch it later.

Now, imagine that this is YOUR event. You are putting it on. You have now done all the things preached about online, offline. Meaning, you are connecting people, offering valuable content, and becoming a trusted resource. Not a bad position to be in, eh?

So—in what creative ways can you assemble the people in your niche?

Speaking

A big benefit of being a trusted resource and community builder is that you can easily turn your content into speeches, discussions, round tables—whatever. Positioning yourself as a speaker as well not only allows you to educate and inspire your audience, it also gives you the chance to introduce people to a slice of your personality. If they want more, they can check out your website later.

You might want to speak for free at first (content resulting in sales), eventually becoming a paid speaker. The world is hungry for more passionate, interesting speakers. I bet you could be one of them.

Think about your niche: What are the organizations that you would like to be in front of? What about conferences? Events? Can you reach out and offer your content as a hand-shake to the event organizer?

Real-life handshakes at events like these are key. Ask pretty much every person used as an example in this book. You see them at conferences and events away from the computer. And often times, they aren't just attending, they are participating in some shape or form.

Tips from Blood, Sweat, and Experience

Over the past few years, I've attended and put on quite a few smarter, faster, cheaper events ranging from Dinner and

Discussions to RISE Lunches to Summer Business Break with the idea of bringing together forward-thinkers, entrepreneurs, marketers, up-and-comers, and so on for a day (or night) filled with fun, new and old connections, and some learning. The funny thing is that the tips here aren't all that different from online content. Because while online and offline are different animals, it is still all about the people—your community and audience. The most successful events mix in all the strategies and ideas in the book:

- It is about others and not you.
- The idea is educate, entertain, and inspire (and offer some handshakes as well).
- The more unique and specific, the better.
- Overcomplicated is a recipe for disaster. Do you really need to hire the flame-throwing, knife jugglers or do you think you can get away without them?
- Give away a present. Is there something people can take home? A prize? A free cookie? A plastic duck?
- Experiment. Try something. Doesn't work that well? Oh well, try something else.
- Utilize your assets to promote it: your website, subscribers, content, and so forth. Let people know what is going on. As your network grows, you have an opportunity to grow your events or keep them small. It is up to you.

By speaking at and dabbling in events, you are increasing your authority and reputation. Plus, by bringing people together, you become the center of relationship building. Seems like time well spent.

Conclusion

At the end of the day, it isn't about technology. Online and offline, it is about becoming a trusted resource and your own version of David. Let Goliath be Goliath.

Rather than requiring more money, it now requires more energy, creativity, and effort.

But it elicits *tremendous* results.

And damn it, if I may say so myself—it is fun and rewarding as well.

The Internet (well, not literally the Internet, since amazing people are the ones developing the tools) has created the tools. More people are spending time online, on social media sites. But this isn't about the technology; it is about people.

One-on-one relationships matter more than ever. And now they are scalable, and it's even easier to access people.

You can't outsource or fake relationships, and it isn't about being everywhere at once. It is about being in the right places at the right times with the right people for you and your business.

Everything here has to do with giving people what they want. In turn, you will get what you want.

This isn't about tricks, or manipulation, or other garbage. It is simply the way the world works. It is based on strategies, ideas, and delicious pieces of information that *actually work*—that are based on real experiences of hundreds of thousands of trusted resources and do-ers and try-ers and experimenters.

The old ways of marketing and promoting businesses are pretty much done. There is a shift going on from faceless companies to ones with vibrant personalities and passion. And instead of product pushers, we have people (not companies) who market and promote by teaching, inspiring, and entertaining.

From product focused to content focused. From mass to one-on-one relationships.

Do it smarter, faster, cheaper. Become that trusted resource for others. And watch your business grow more than you ever could have imagined as a result.

About the Author

Entrepreneur, mediapreneur, speaker, and author David Siteman Garland is the founder of *The Rise To The Top*, The #1 Non-Boring Resource For Building Your Business Smarter, Faster, Cheaper. He writes and hosts *RISE*, a Web show for entrepreneurs and forward thinkers, as well as *The Rise To The Top TV* show on ABC.

His philosophy is simple: Money follows passion and not the other way around.

After starting and stopping several unique entrepreneurial adventures and dabbling in everything from radio to hockey, David became frustrated that he could not find a great resource (that wasn't a snoozefest) where people could learn about building, marketing, and promoting their own businesses from experienced and unique entrepreneurs who could talk from experience as opposed to fluffy theory. People doing it by being smarter, faster, cheaper as opposed to dumber, slower, and expensive. What was missing was a new series of shows that could be both entertaining and educational and part of a larger online hub that would resonate with forward-thinking entrepreneurs.

Because such a show and website did not exist, David decided to build them himself. Investing all of his savings, time, and energy, he created—from scratch—a TV show, a series of

Web shows, an online resource, and a vibrant community of entrepreneurs.

Like many ventures, *The Rise To The Top* was born through brainstorming in a coffee shop. David shared his idea for the show with friends, successful business owners, and creative types, all of whom thought it was a great concept. *The Rise To The Top* quickly attracted a wide and varied fan base, including not only the targeted demographic of young entrepreneurs but also more "mature" (young-at-heart) viewers.

The shows and Web resource now have over 100,000 monthly viewers, with a big focus on interviews that pick the brains of top entrepreneurs, forward thinkers, and authors including Gary Vaynerchuk (Wine Library), Chris Brogan (ChrisBrogan.com), Tony Hsieh (Zappos), The Millionaire Matchmaker Patti Stanger, Seth Godin, and many others.

David has been featured on CNN, ABC, NBC, CBS, City TV, My Network Television, as well as on KMOX and in *Alive Magazine, The Riverfront Times, Ladue News*, and *St. Louis Magazine*. He has no idea why he has become a media magnet so early in his career, but he's certainly not turning down interviews and fun opportunities.

David has contributed as a writer and business/ entrepreneurial/marketing commentator to CNN, CBS BNET, Small Business Trends, *The St. Louis Business Journal*, Personal Branding Blog, *Speaker Magazine, Small Business Monthly*, and *Great Day St. Louis*. He was recently selected by *Speaker Magazine* as one of the Hot Speakers of the Year.

David has also guest lectured at Washington University in St. Louis, St. Louis University, and Fontbonne University. He lives in exotic St. Louis, Missouri, and always loves to hear from readers. You can reach him on Twitter (twitter.com/ therisetothetop), Facebook (facebook.com/risetothetop), and via e-mail at David@DSGagency.com.

Index